GETTING AWAY WITH MURDER

THE LIFE AND TIMES
OF
OLIVER MILTON LEE
NEW MEXICO CATTLEMAN, CONGRESSMAN, AND KILLER

GETTING AWAY WITH MURDER

The Life and Times
of
Oliver Milton Lee
New Mexico Cattleman, Congressman, and Killer

W. C. Jameson

Santa Fe

Sunstone books may be purchased for educational, business, or sales promotional use.
For information please write: Special Markets Department, Sunstone Press,
P.O. Box 2321, Santa Fe, New Mexico 87504-2321.

Printed on acid-free paper

♾

eBook: 978-1-61139-791-8

Library of Congress Cataloging-in-Publication Data

Names: Jameson, W. C., 1942- author
Title: Getting away with murder : the life and times of Oliver Milton Lee New Mexico cattleman, congressman, and killer / W. C. Jameson.
Description: Santa Fe, NM : Sunstone Press, [2025] | Includes bibliographical references. | Summary: "The Life and Times of Oliver Milton Lee, New Mexico Cattleman, Congressman, and Killer"-- Provided by publisher.
Identifiers: LCCN 2026005753 | ISBN 9781632937841 paperback | ISBN 9781632937858 hardcover | ISBN 9781611397918 epub
Subjects: LCSH: Lee, Oliver, 1865-1941 | Garrett, Pat F. (Pat Floyd), 1850-1908 | Fountain, Albert Jennings, 1838-1896 | Frontier and pioneer life--New Mexico | New Mexico--History--1848- | New Mexico | LCGFT: Biographies
Classification: LCC F801 .J36 2025 | DDC 978.9/04--dc23/eng/20260206
LC record available at https://lccn.loc.gov/2026005753

WWW.SUNSTONEPRESS.COM
SUNSTONE PRESS / POST OFFICE BOX 2321 / SANTA FE, NM 87504-2321 /USA
(505) 988-4418

CONTENTS

INTRODUCTION

The brochure for a popular state park established in 1980 and nestled in the foothills of the Sacramento Mountains in the southern part of New Mexico states that it was "named for Oliver Milton Lee, a pioneer...rancher and state legislator...." What the brochure does not relate is that Oliver Lee was also a killer, a man whose sense of physical and economic survival led him to the planning and execution of plots to kill Albert Jennings Fountain, an influential and prominent soldier, newspaperman, politician, and judge, as well as Pat Garrett, at the time one of the most famous and visible lawmen in the country. Though Oliver Lee was responsible for the deaths of several men, the killings of Fountain and Garrett, both shrouded in controversy and mystery, have been regarded as among the most sensational assassinations in the history of the American West. In addition, Lee either killed or masterminded the killings of others, including a cattle detective, an El Paso constable, ranchers, and cowhands. In every case, Lee got away with murder.

Oliver Milton Lee is a name unknown to most Americans in spite of the fact that he played a significant role in the settlement of a vast portion of New Mexico, was regarded as one of the state's original successful ranchers, was heralded as a statesman, and elected to the state's legislature on six different occasions.

Though operating outside the law for most of his life, it was said of Lee that he had a strong sense of justice. In his mind, however, law and justice were not necessarily the same thing, at least not as it related to himself. It was also agreed that Lee, fed up with the laws and the legal system existing in southern New Mexico, sought his own kind of justice. He also believed he was strong enough and influential enough to achieve it, regardless of the odds. History has proven him correct.

Though the following pages focus on Oliver Milton Lee, this book is about much more: It is about a time and place where powerful men got away with inflicting their own interpretation of the law onto their fellow citizens to benefit themselves and their co-conspirators; it is about how corrupt politicians and lawyers, along with inadequate and incompetent law enforcement, shaped history and generated mysteries that have baffled observers and historians for generations.

Until now, following the discovery of documents and information never before seen, or was misinterpreted, by previous writers, the long-baffling mysteries associated with the assassinations of Albert Jennings Fountain and Pat Garret have been solved, with the names of the participants and the circumstances revealed. The materials also shed light on Oliver Milton Lee, long an overlooked figure in the history and settlement of the American Southwest, but a man who nevertheless had a profound influence and impact. Lee was a successful man on many levels, including cattle rancher and politician. Lee achieved these successes by dint of hard work and commitment, but also by eliminating his competition by killing them.

1
ORIGINS

Mary Hendrick Lee was a "stocky, courageous woman with snapping black eyes," according to author C. L. Sonnichsen. She grew up in Burnet County, Texas, during a time of intense feuding and violence, and married a man named Altman with whom she had a son, Perry. Altman died when Perry was seven. Mary later took up with a man who came from New York named Lee and eventually married him. Lee had earlier gone to California during the gold rush to seek his fortune. Like many others, however, his quest was a failed one and he decided to try his luck elsewhere. The trail took him Burnet County, Texas, where he met and married the widow Altman. In Burnet County, he and Mary raised cattle and horses on a small ranch. They had a son, Oliver Milton Lee, born on October 31, 1865. Oliver would grow to become a significant element and powerful force in late nineteenth century and early twentieth century New Mexico history, and would factor into a number of pivotal historical events.

In time, the Lee family moved to Buffalo Gap, Texas, in Taylor County where they continued to raise livestock. At the time, Buffalo Gap, located fifteen miles southwest of Abilene, was little more than the name of a geographical location and the setting for a tiny, almost insignificant settlement. While there, the Lee family operated a successful ranch raising cattle and horses. At an early age, Oliver demonstrated an uncommon ability with horses and cattle, particularly the former. Due to his skill with and dedication to livestock, the family accumulated a fine herd of horses.

As he grew into a man, Oliver Lee was described as "good looking and charming" and he neither drank nor smoked. At nineteen years of age he was considered handsome, yet shy, though greatly admired by the girls who knew him. It was said that during this time Lee preferred spending his time with livestock rather than in what he regarded as the silly pursuits related to courting. According to Sonnichsen, Lee was "magnificently muscled, straight as a young pine, [and] catlike in his coordination." He also inherited his mother's piercing black eyes which seemed to bore into men. In spite of his sometimes intimidating appearance, Lee spoke softly and was generally courteous.

During the early 1880s, the area around Taylor County was hit by a severe drought, one that had a dramatic effect on area ranchers and farmers. Not wishing to lose any more of their cattle and horses to the dry spell, the Lee family determined it was time to relocate. Sons Oliver and Perry traveled to New Mexico to look for a suitable location to establish a ranch.

During the early to mid-1880s, a number of Texas cattlemen were seeking to relocate, and the Territory of New Mexico offered promise. Herds from 200 to 400 head of cattle arrived and were placed on public domain land. Cattlemen who could afford it shipped their stock to El Paso, Texas, via rail and then moved them onto the available lands. Less affluent ranchers were forced to herd their cattle overland. According to author A. M. Gibson:

> ...these Texans, a special breed—insolent, high-tempered,
> and intensely loyal—raised hell. They brought to New
> Mexico their curious folkways, open range ranching,
> community roundups, and abundant trouble for anyone
> who dared cross them."

During their search for ranchland, Oliver and Perry encountered Bill Kelham (sometimes spelled Kellam), who owned a small spread near the tiny community of Ruidoso.

Kelham, who was nicknamed Cherokee Bill, informed the brothers that he knew of a choice piece of land on the west side of the Sacramento Mountains with good water. He told the boys that the location was occupied by a man known as Frenchy, who raised cattle and goats, but that he might be willing to sell. Kelham agreed to take them to look over the property.

After examining the land adjacent to the Sacramento Mountains, Oliver and Perry determined that it suited their needs. The brothers began making plans to move the family and the livestock. They rode back to Buffalo Gap and related their findings to their parents. During the early spring of 1885, Oliver and Perry returned to New Mexico with their herds of horses and cattle, their mother and father, and two black ranch hands named Eph and Ed.

Though the land at the foothills of the Sacramento Mountains was rough, dry, and challenging, it supported a healthy growth of hardy grasses and proved suitable, even promising, for ranching. A stream of fine spring water flowed out of Dog Canyon, a deep and picturesque cut in the range. In time, the elder Lee died, and the operation of the ranch fell into the hands of Oliver and Perry.

Oliver had not yet turned twenty years of age. He was keenly interested in matching the family's livestock to this new land with the confidence that both would thrive. During this time, Lee demonstrated a keen ability with both rifle and handgun and was regarded by many as an excellent marksman. A story was told that Lee was able to toss a half-dollar into the air, fire his revolver, and hit it without even seeming to aim. Another tale recalled that Lee and some friends set up a pine board a mile distant for target practice. Lee was said to have hit it five shots out of six with a rifle.

Among the newly arrived rough-hewn, brazen, clannish, and proud Texas cattlemen who settled in and near the Tularosa Basin, Oliver Lee emerged as a leader. He soon established the Circle Cross brand for his cattle and the Double S for his horses.

As a young man, Oliver Lee expressed an interest in "getting ahead," in expanding his ranch and his herds. He was hard working, ambitious, and unafraid, all qualities essential to succeeding in a challenging landscape.

The family grew. Brother Perry Altman traveled back to Buffalo Gap, Texas, to marry his sweetheart. He soon returned with her to New Mexico and the couple moved into a house he built eight miles west of Tularosa. Oliver continued to live with his mother and her niece, Nettie Fry, whom she raised in a two-room adobe structure on the flats some twenty miles from White Sands and due west of Dog Canyon. White Sands was an expanse of dunes composed of fine grains and pale in appearance as a result of having been derived from weathered gypsum. Today it is a national monument. Lee drilled a well on the new property, the first between Ysleta, Texas, and La Luz, New Mexico, and put up a windmill. The location was, and is, known as Lee's well.

The little family was soon joined by George McDonald. Like the rest of the Lee clan, McDonald was from Burnet County, Texas, and initially joined the family at Buffalo Gap. When the decision was made to move to New Mexico, McDonald accompanied them. McDonald's choice to join the Lees was two-fold. First, he and Nettie had grown close and planned to get married. Second, George and Oliver grew up together, were nearly inseparable, and carried on as brothers. They talked often together about their goals, the conversations invariably involving a discussion of ways to get ahead.

The Lees and the Altmans corresponded with friends in Texas, recommending the setting and potential opportunities in New Mexico. In a short time, they were joined by the McNews, Raleys, and Gillilands. McNew and Gilliland became what author A.M. Gibson termed "hard core Lee partisans," who were soon joined by Bill Carr and Tom Tucker. Each of these men had previous brushes with the law, including rustling and murder. They were tough men in a tough country. They were fearless, and could be violent at times, characteristics often related to survival in this young country. In time, men would die at the hands of these riders.

Olivier Milton Lee

2
CONFRONTATION

Throughout his lifetime, Oliver Lee was a participant in a number of confrontations, most of them violent. As far as can be determined, the first showdown of any consequence he experienced was with a neighboring rancher named John Good. Good owned a great deal of ranchland in the region and occupied much of his time trying to obtain more. His brand, known to everybody in the area, was **7HL** connected. As a result of his position and success in the ranching community, Good wielded a significant amount of power and he knew it. He was used to getting his way, and as far as he was concerned, nothing was going to change that. It was inevitable that Lee and Good would collide.

Oliver Lee located a small spring near the foothills of the Sacramento Mountains. The spring was close to the family ranch land, but not within the property line. Oliver and George McDonald dug out the spring, rocked it up, and created a small pool of water, something handy for their livestock and for any thirsty cowhand who happened to pass by. In time, Lee traded this spring to another neighbor, L. S. Reynolds. Before the spring was traded to Reynolds, however, it created a problem between Lee and Good.

Not far from the spring, John Good had a large earthen tank that he kept filled with water for his cattle as a result of a pipeline that stretched from Tularosa to this location. Lee was aware of Good's tank, and made certain his own cattle never wandered in that direction. When John Good learned what Lee had done relative to developing the tiny spring, he grew incensed and determined to deliver instructions on how things were done in that part of the country, or more precisely, how John Good wanted them done.

Good found Lee and McDonald out on the range one day and spurred his horse up to them. He told the two young men he had found out what they had done and ordered them to move on and stay away from his land and water. He informed them he had come to this range first and was not going to put up with anyone else's cattle at his tank.

McDonald, who was reputed to have a short fuse and a hot temper, grew angry. He told Good he was not afraid of him and warned him about trying to run him and Oliver off. Good repeated his warning, turned his mount, and rode away.

Lee and McDonald were well aware of Good's reputation. A few months earlier, a cattleman named Charlie Dawson got into an argument with Good over a business deal. The argument devolved into shouting and threats. Before Dawson left, the two men agreed that the next time they met up, they would shoot it out. It was not long before it happened.

Dawson and Good encountered one another on the streets of La Luz on December 8, 1865. They immediately drew their weapons and proceeded to shoot at one another. Dawson went down, wounded from one of Good's bullets. Good, untouched, walked away.

Lee and McDonald encountered Good from time to time during trips to town. McDonald invariably took the opportunity to tell Good what he thought of him and refused to back away from the older rancher's threats and blustering. Good, always quick to anger, would be on the verge of hurling more threats when McDonald would simply turn and walk away, leaving Good cursing and spitting. It was clear to anyone observing these goings-on that matters would eventually come to a head. That time finally arrived one day in 1888.

It was roundup time during the fall of that year, an occasion when neighboring ranchers got together, gathered up all of the cattle they could find, separated them out according to brands, and marked the calves. Bill Earhart, an employee of the Jim Cooper ranch, had been designated roundup boss for this season. Not long before the gathering was to take place, Earhart had been working for John Good, but the two men had a falling out. As roundup boss, Earhart approached Good to ask how many hands he would spare to help with the roping and branding. Good said he wasn't sending any, but that he would instruct a contingent of his men to cut his **7HL** cattle out of the gathering.

Earhart, a man of little patience and short of temper, was known as one to never back away from a fight. He cursed Good and told him if he didn't send a crew to help, he would not be allowed to cut his stock from the main herd.

Good warned Earhart that if any **7HL** cattle were rounded up, it should be clear to everyone who they belonged to. He told the roundup boss that he would be coming after his cattle. Earhart, realizing Good was getting the better of the argument, finally told the rancher that he could come and get his cattle, but that he had to wait until everyone else had made their cut. Earhart warned Good not to arrive any sooner.

During the roundup, Earhart appointed Wat Gilmore, barely in his teens, to keep a watch and shout a warning if any of John Good's cowhands showed up. It wasn't long before Gilmore spotted six riders approaching and informed Earhart. Earhart recognized the oncoming group as Good's ranch hands, and noted that they were led by Walter Good, John's son. Earhart warned the other cowboys, and suggested they arm themselves. The hands went to the cook wagon where their weapons were stored and retrieved them.

Walter Good was described as a lanky, left-handed cowboy who was proficient with a rope and with cutting horses. He also had a reputation of being worthless and no- account, a troublemaker. Walter, accompanied by the other **7HL** ranch hands, rode up to Earhart. If Walter had any notions of presenting demands, it is likely he was swayed by the presence of the armed cowboys and Earhart's confident manner. Earhart tersely informed Walter that he needed to stay away from the herd until he was given permission to return and claim **7HL** cattle.

As the two men spoke, Walter spotted George McDonald heating a branding iron in preparation for marking a calf that was being held down by two cowboys. Though he was a significant distance from the activity, Walter insisted to McDonald that it was a **7HL** calf that he was getting ready to brand. How he knew this, if he did, has never been explained. Good ordered McDonald to mark it with a **7HL** brand.

McDonald informed Good it was a maverick, but that it had been following a cow with the Cooper brand, the Triangle T, and he was going to put the Cooper brand on the calf. That said, he proceeded to brand the calf.

Fuming, Good turned his horse and rode away, the **7HL** ranch hands following behind. He rode straight to his father and told him what he had seen. John Good had already been close to feuding with rancher Jim Cooper, and this most recent incident did nothing to allay his antagonism toward the man.

Jim Cooper had been raised with his two brothers near Jacksboro, Texas. His father was the town physician. When Jim Cooper dropped out of school at Denison, Texas, Dr. Cooper provided him with several head of cattle and horses so that he could start his own ranch. Cooper herded his stock and transported his belongings to Colorado City, Texas, where he succeeded in building a sizeable herd of cattle.

In 1883, Cooper had heard about the possibilities of good ranchland in New Mexico, particularly in the area of Tularosa. With little delay, he moved his cattle, some 3,000 head. With him came his brother Clay and friend Bill Earhart. Earhart was regarded as Cooper's partner.

Cooper took to this part of New Mexico readily. He was sociable and agreeable, but strong, determined, and hard working. He could play the fiddle, a popular talent at the time, and was good at business.

About a year after arriving, Cooper realized he had more cattle than he had grass and water for them. He learned that his neighbor John Good had plenty of both and sought to enter into a partnership with him. The partnership cattle carried the **LO** brand, about 2,000 head. The agreement between the two men went smoothly for two years, and then trouble started.

John Good often paid his cowhands with cattle, but the animals he turned over to them came not from his own herd but from the **LO** bunch. Cooper expressed his displeasure with this arrangement, and the partnership began to unravel. By the time of the roundup headed by Bill Earhart, Cooper and Good had ended their arrangement and barely spoke to one another. Tensions rose, heated, and were about to reach a boiling point.

As the drama between John Good and others simmered and grew, Oliver Lee observed from a distance. Lee suspected that he and John Good were destined for a face-off in the near future. It was not long in coming.

3
MURDER

Not long after the massive roundup was over, George McDonald was murdered. After eating his dinner early one evening, McDonald left his cabin and walked up into a nearby canyon to check on his water supply, a spring that emanated from the wall of the canyon. After looking over the spring and clearing debris from the pool, McDonald reclined in the cool shade of the canyon, his back against a rock, and spent some time braiding a quirt. From behind a boulder thirty feet away, a man rose up and fired a rifle, the bullet striking McDonald in the center of his forehead, passing though his skull, and flattening against the rock.

McDonald's body was found later by Benito Montoya while he and several cowhands were hunting for lost cattle. One of the cowboys, Tom McDonald, said George died instantly "without a struggle, nor even moving his feet, which were crossed, or turning his head." The position of the body suggested that George never attempted to reach for his revolver.

The cowboys found the tracks of a horse that they suspected had been ridden by the killer. They followed the tracks out of the canyon all the way to Tularosa Canyon. Once there, all trace of it was lost.

One interesting observation was noted by the trackers. During the murderer's flight, his horse ran squarely into a tough, spiked leaf of a Spanish dagger, a particularly durable desert plant of the yucca family. A triangular piece of the horse's hide was still stuck to the spike. Later, it was said that the piece of horsehide fit perfectly into an injury suffered by a horse belonging to Walter Good.

Even without the piece of incriminating horsehide, most people already suspected Walter Good as McDonald's killer, which by extension involved John Good. Discussion revolved around whether Walter Good actually pulled the trigger or if the assassination had been carried out by one of his ranch hands named José Espalin. Espalin had been linked to another assassination two years earlier, but he was never charged. Others were convinced that a hired gun was brought in from Texas, a man who returned to that state once the job was completed. It was said the Texas man was later arrested and brought to Las Cruces for a trial. The judge was forced to turn him loose, however, when no one could be found to testify against him.

After McDonald's murder, Cooper took a stand with Oliver Lee and against John Good. Lee was deeply shaken by McDonald's murder. He had lost his best friend, and his feelings toward the Goods, already hardened, grew intense. According to family members, Lee retrieved the flattened bullet that killed McDonald from the rock and carried it around with him on the end of his watch chain as a reminder. Lee could sense greater troubles in the future between him and the Goods, and he knew he would have to prepare.

4
REVENGE

Walter Good was a marked man. Despite what turned out to be a plethora of suspects mentioned in the death of George McDonald, most of the attention was directed toward Walter. More than any other, Oliver Lee was convinced that Walter was the man who pulled the trigger on his friend, and was determined to do something about it. He, along with Perry Altman, began making plans for revenge.

On Monday, August 13, 1888, Perry Altman rode up to Walter Good's house to inform him that a paint horse that belonged to him had wandered into his, Altman's, pasture. Altman told Good he had been watering it, but that if he wanted his horse back, he needed to come and get it. Good said he would come out in the morning and retrieve the horse.

The next morning, Tuesday, August 14, 1888, Walter Good rode out of his yard on his way to the Altman place. It was the last time any of his family members saw him alive. On Wednesday morning, Walter's brother-in-law, Hugh Taylor, arrived at the Altman place. He located Perry and told him that John Good was growing concerned over the whereabouts of his son and was trying to locate him. Altman said he didn't know anything about where Walter Good might be.

By mid-afternoon, at least fifty men, many of them John Good's ranch hands, were riding throughout the flats and foothills in search of Walter. Perry Altman even joined them.

Needless to say, John Good was deeply troubled by the disappearance of his son and suspected foul play. His suspicions immediately focused on Oliver Lee, Jim Cooper, Perry Altman, and a man named Tom Tucker, a sometime Lee ranch hand and a survivor of Arizona's bloody Graham-Tewksbury feud. The kindling of his suspicions turned into a raging fire when he learned from an informant that Lee, Cooper, and Tucker had all met at Altman's house the evening before Walter disappeared. Good was convinced the stray horse story was a ruse to lure Walter to the Altman place where they intended harm.

John Good approached a La Luz Justice of the Peace—Humphrey Hill—and talked him into swearing out warrants for the arrests of Lee, Altman, Cooper, and Tucker for carrying weapons. Hill put together a small posse, of which Good was a member, and went in search of the suspects. Lee, Cooper, and Tucker were nowhere to be found, but Altman was taken into custody and transported back to town for questioning. John Good took the suspect into a back room and spent almost the entire night raging and threatening. Altman weathered the storm, but just before dawn Good suggested they take him out and hang him. He was talked out of it by Hugh Taylor, Walter's brother-in-law. Altman was released a short time later.

Oliver Lee and John Good were now both well aware they were embroiled in a struggle, if not a war. Both men, along with their ranch hands, carried weapons. When Lee or Good showed up in town, residents scattered, doing their best to remove themselves from a potential line of fire. Good offered a reward of $300 for the return of son Walter, dead or alive. Finally convinced that Walter was dead, he also posted a reward of $1,000 for the arrest and conviction of his son's murderers.

In the company of several of his hired men, Good rode his and adjacent ranges day and night in search of Lee, Cooper, and Tucker. His stated intention was to kill them on sight. Whether as a result of removing themselves from Good's growing wrath or merely going on a hunting trip, the three men had been camping in the Agua Chiquita Mountains located a few miles to the north. According to the *Rio Grande Republican*, a Las Cruces newspaper, the Good and Lee factions were responsible for "a reign of terror [that] has not been known since the Lincoln County War."

Several dozen La Luz citizens, suffering a decline in business and fearing for their lives, submitted a petition to county sheriff Guadalupe Ascarate demanding he see to it that the Lee and Good factions were disarmed. Ascarate, perceived by many to be a weak law enforcement officer, left his Las Cruces headquarters for La Luz, three miles north of Alamogordo, but claimed he was never able to locate any of the participants in the growing feud.

With the situation becoming desperate and threatening, a few of the more nervous citizens simply packed up and left. Charley Graham, Oliver Lee's brother-in-law, loaded his family and belongings into a wagon and moved to a new place in the foothills of the San Mateo Mountains, two hundred miles to the northwest.

Somehow word reached Lee and his companions in the mountains that Good was searching for them, and that there were warrants for their arrest. Lee sent a message stating that they would not surrender to local law enforcement officials, that he could not trust them to provide adequate protection.

John Good not only did not let up in his search for Lee *et al*, he intensified it. Lee determined that should he and his friends eventually have an encounter with Good that they were woefully underequipped—they had only a small supply of ammunition. Lee, meanwhile, in the company of Altman, departed his hiding place in the mountains and traveled to El Paso where the two purchased additional arms as well as at least two five-gallon cans filled with ammunition.

Meanwhile, Good and his ranch hands were stalking the residences of the men they pursued. Eph, the black man who worked for the Lees as well as for the recently departed Charley Graham, reported that at least one prowler, believed to be one of Good's posse members, had made his way to the roof of the recently vacated Graham house where Eph was staying.

On returning from a trip to El Paso, Emma Altman, Perry's wife, found her home burned to the ground. When she arrived, she discovered deputy sheriff E. C. Rucker and his posse, which included another of John Good's sons, Charley, moving around the ruined house and excavating holes under what had once been the wooden floor. Emma also discovered someone had shot her little dog. Deputy Rucker was a staunch supporter of John Good, and even worked for him at one time. When Emma asked what they were doing, Rucker replied that they were looking for Walter Good's body.

Rucker and his men were operating on a lead that may have been nothing more than gossip. Days earlier while Emma Altman was scrubbing her floors, a neighbor dropped by to visit. Later while in town, the neighbor offered the story that Emma had been scrubbing at bloodstains and that the body of Walter Good was at that moment lying under her bed wrapped in a bed sheet.

Oliver Lee wasted no time in denouncing John Good as being behind the burning of Perry Altman's house. In turn, Good claimed Lee and his men torched the structure in order to eliminate evidence related to the death of Walter.

As if the tale of Walter Good wrapped in a bed sheet and stuffed under Altman's bed was not grisly enough, another story making the rounds had Walter tied to one of the corral fence posts where he was beaten and then shot. It was claimed that on examination, one could find bullet holes in the post, along with shreds of Walter's shirt and bits of hair. As a result, Rucker's men dug holes in the corral and inspected all of the posts. Nothing was found.

Two days later around two o'clock in the afternoon, Walter Good, or at least what remained of him, was found. A party consisting of fifteen men and led by John Good had been searching the White Sands area for most of the day. A desiccated body—mostly a skeleton—had been found in the dunes. Walter Good had been dead for approximately two weeks and his body had been ravaged by coyotes, buzzards, and other carrion-eaters. The corpse was identified from the clothes and boots that remained, as well as some jewelry Walter was known to wear. Two bullet holes were found in Walter's left temple. In the mind of John Good, as well as many others, the killing was connected to Oliver Lee. It would not be the last time a killing in the White Sands would be associated with Lee.

Most of the searchers departed for their homes save for five of them—Good's cowhands. Good led the way back to the ranch where he intended to communicate the news of the discovery. Following that, he planned to contact the county sheriff to recover Walter's body and conduct an investigation. They were unprepared for the trouble they were about to encounter.

As Good and his men topped a low rise not far from his ranch headquarters, they were ambushed by five men who had taken cover behind a ditch bank about one hundred yards away. The ambushers were Oliver Lee, Perry Altman, Bill Earhart, Tom Tucker, and Bill Kelham. Finding themselves at a disadvantage, Good and his men attempted to hide in a nearby cornfield.

According to a September 18, 1888 edition of the *Rio Grande Republican,* over one hundred shots were fired with no one getting hit. Two horses were killed, however, and a third suffered a wound.

After the gunfight was over, Good rode straight to La Luz and informed Deputy Sheriff Nicolas Armijo of the discovery of Walter's body and the firefight with Oliver Lee and his men near the ranch. Armijo immediately sent for Sheriff Ascarate at Las Cruces, sixty miles to the southwest. Ascarate, accompanied by a posse of twenty-five men, arrived at

La Luz the following day. A number of the posse members, led by Deputy Rucker, were sent to retrieve Walter's body.

The next day, a coroner's jury was formed and somehow arrived at the conclusion that Walter Good met his death at the hands of Oliver Lee, Jim Cooper, Bill Kelham, and Tom Tucker. Walter Good was buried on the morning of September 7, 1888, on the ranch where he grew up, the service conducted by the Reverend Adolfo Cardenas.

With Lee and his associates formally charged with killing Walter Good, things became even more tense. The wives and mothers of the Lee clan all moved in with Oliver's mother. When not working the cattle, Lee and his men hid in the deserts and mountains at night, never telling their women where they were. They left word that they would surrender peacefully to proper authorities, but not to men who were little more than puppets for John Good. For his part, the timid Sheriff Ascarate wanted nothing to do with the Lee bunch and stayed away. While Lee and company were in hiding, people from town would arrive at his house informing the women of plots being hatched to have them killed.

Then came the news that the women would be gathered up and taken to La Luz for questioning. Not long afterward, deputy sheriff Rucker arrived at the Lee residence with a large posse. The elder Mrs. Lee spotted the lawmen from a distance and hastily escorted all of the women out of the house and to a hiding place behind a windmill.

Mrs. Lee returned to the house, locked all of the doors and windows, and stepped out onto the front porch to greet the deputy and his men who had reined up their horses just outside the fence. Rucker pulled a paper from his pocket and, oddly, proceeded to read its contents to Mrs. Lee in Spanish. Mrs. Lee stopped him and told him to go get papers that were written in English.

As Mrs. Lee spoke to Rucker, another deputy started to guide his horse through an opening in the fence and head toward the windmill. Mrs. Lee ordered him to stay back and asked him what he wanted. He told her he just wanted a drink of water for himself and his horse. She told him to go drink out of a nearby horse trough. Presently, the deputies turned and rode back to La Luz.

During the nights when the men were hiding out, the women could hear voices and footsteps out in the yard. The women had no guns, but they collected all of the knives and axes and kept them nearby in the event they were attacked.

Presently, Lee sent word to friend Charles W. Moore, a Tularosa resident, that he and his companions were going to surrender themselves to the authorities. Lee told Moore that they were coming in on the evening of September 7, and asked him to meet them and assume responsibility for their welfare. Moore met the fugitives at a pre-arranged location and led them to the home of Patrick Coghlan (sometimes spelled Coughlin). Visitors to the Coghlan place were in awe of Lee and his men, fitted as they were with arms and ammunition. They further marveled at what author Sonnichsen referred to as "their carefree demeanor, and the nerve they showed in coming to town at all." While supper was being prepared, Jim Cooper pulled a fiddle down from the wall and entertained the Coghlin company with a selection of jigs and reels.

The following morning, Moore led Lee, Cooper, Tucker, and Altman down the road toward Las Cruces. Each man was sensitive to any potential problem they might encounter along the way, and as they rode they scanned the surrounding landscape on the lookout for riders. Trouble was not long in coming.

During a stop in Tularosa, Charles W. Moore had a message sent to John Good informing him that they were on the road to Las Cruces to meet with the authorities. The message went on to say that if Good had any intention of traveling that same road to please wait until the Lee party had passed in order to avoid any trouble.

Lee *et al* set out on that road Saturday night and arrived at Lee's Well the next morning where they napped for two hours and changed horses. After covering another twenty miles they arrived at the home of a man named Forrester where they took dinner.

Throughout the entire journey, the Lee party saw no indication that anyone was following them, however, during the meal they learned that deputy sheriff Rucker was leading a large posse in pursuit. A short time later when the posse came in sight, Lee spotted John Good at the head of it. Good or Rucker sent a message to Lee telling him to resume their journey. Thinking that Good and the posse wanted to get their quarry out in the open where they could ambush them or engage them in a gunfight, Lee sent a return message instructing the posse not to crowd them and explained that they were going to Las Cruces to turn themselves in.

After the meal, the Lee party mounted up and set out once again on the road to Las Cruces. After riding ten miles, they grew suspicious of an ambush or trap. They left the road and decided to remain in a secluded camp for a few days, but no more trouble was forthcoming. Only Cooper, Earhart, and Altman rode into Las Cruces in the company of two-dozen or more friends they enlisted as escorts and surrendered to the authorities. For their defense, they hired two legal firms, Waddil and Young, along with Newcomb and McFie.

Lee and Tucker were determined to remain in hiding until they learned what happened with their companions. Lee had long harbored a distrust for law enforcement, as well as lawyers, and was unwilling to turn himself in until he was completely aware of current circumstances. Lee wanted a situation that he could control. His companions were now in the custody of the sheriff, and therefore had forfeited control. Events began to unfold and matters grew more tense.

Perry Altman

5
OUTCOME

Perry Altman, Jim Cooper, and Bill Earhart were sequestered in the Las Cruces jail for several days. During the first week of October they, along with Oliver Lee and Bill Kelham, were indicted for murder. Bond was raised and posted for Cooper, Altman, and Earhart and they left the courtroom, free to move about the countryside as they chose. Oliver Lee had yet to surrender to the authorities and effectively avoided all attempts to locate him.

With Lee, Cooper, and friends loose, the area citizenry waited to see when the next round of fighting would occur. Rumors emanating from El Paso held that the Good and Lee factions, all armed and anxious, were on the verge of a final battle. The September 15, 1889 edition of the *Rio Grande Republican* quoted a column from the Lincoln *Independent* that stated "unless some determined men take a hand to prevent further outrage and murders, it seems probable that the present guerilla warfare will be continued between the Cooper and Good factions until one or both are exterminated."

One day in early December, John Good and a crew of ranch hands were out rounding up some horses when they encountered Jim Cooper riding with some friends. The two sides met on the road and confronted one another. One of Good's cowboys yanked a rifle from a saddle scabbard as Cooper neared. Cooper glared at the man and warned him not to do anything short of putting the weapon away. The cowboy complied. A second cowhand drew a pistol and pointed it at Cooper, but Lee Good, one of John's nephews, slapped the gun barrel down and instructed the cowboy to re-holster it. John Good, who was astride his horse at the front of the contingent of ranch hands, turned in his saddle and ordered everyone to calm down. This was the first break in Good's normally aggressive and threatening demeanor. The likely truth was, John Good, still suffering from the loss of his son, Walter, had grown weary of the fighting; it had worn him down and was clearly affecting his health.

After observing from a distance how the process for Cooper and the others had progressed, Lee and Tucker rode into Las Cruces and gave themselves up. They were admitted to bail at $10,000 each and turned loose for the time being. During the hearing in the courtroom, Lee and an assistant prosecutor named Albert Jennings Fountain encountered one another for the first time. The hostilities between the two men would simmer and eventually grow into a white-hot intensity.

During testimony at the hearing, according to an article in the *Rio Grande Republican*, Eph, the black man who had come to New Mexico with the Lees and who was most recently working for Charley Graham, testified under oath that he had witnessed Walter Good being murdered in Perry Altman's corral. During a subsequent trial, Eph denied he had ever stated such.

In a move that was at the time quite uncharacteristic of Good, he invited Cooper's brother Ira to travel to La Luz and assist in making an effort to reestablish peace and harmony in the area. Ira agreed to come. A short time later, John Good appeared as though he was ready to give in and give up. During the middle of December, he leased out his five-hundred-acre ranch near La Luz, along with a larger piece of ranchland, to Tularosa citizen C. P. White. Not long afterward, Good abandoned his home and moved to Las Cruces where he lived in a rented house. The venerable John Good had given up ranching, the only thing he knew. In doing so, he had finally given in to Oliver Lee and Jim Cooper. In time, Good even left Las Cruces.

Months later, Tom McDonald encountered Good in Deming, New Mexico, then again later in Arizona. The last news of John Good to reach the Tularosa area had him in Oklahoma in the employ of another. He was broke and nearly destitute.

Months passed after their surrender and neither Oliver Lee nor any of his cohorts were brought to trial for cattle rustling. In 1889, the court venue was switched to Socorro County. A trial was scheduled, then postponed. Bertha Good, the wife of John, was likewise weary of all the conflict and animosity and had one of the suits her husband had filed dismissed. Eventually, the entire matter died from lack of action and interest.

On March 10, 1896, a letter written by Pinkerton Detective agent James McPharland to New Mexico Governor W. T. Thornton he stated that "...one Walter Good was killed by Oliver Lee, Tom Tucker, Bill Kelham, known as Cherokee Bill, and his body was buried in what is known as White Sands...."

According to author Sonnichsen:

> This was the first and perhaps the only time that Lee, Cooper, and Company had tried to make Range Law and Town Law agree, only to find that it couldn't be done. This was the first of many experiences which convinced them that there was little justice available for their kind in court procedure. The standards they lived by were too often in conflict with the other set of rules; acts which to them seemed just and right were crimes on the statute books. Nine times out of ten they came before them not as accusers but as accused; and they learned that survival for such as they meant circumventing the district attorney.

The feud between John Good and the Lee-Cooper faction was apparently over, and the region around Tularosa, to a great degree, returned to normal. To observers, it was clear that Oliver Lee was the victor.

Jim Cooper married Bonnie Brazel of the Brazel ranching family in 1890. Cooper was convinced his future in ranching lay in the plains area near Magdalena, New Mexico, and relocated his family and livestock there. Unfortunately for him, as well as other ranchers, a severe drought struck the region and destroyed their enterprises. Cooper eventually moved to Oklahoma, and in his later years served as the president of a bank. He died in 1937.

Perry Altman moved back to Texas, eventually settling in Crow Flats, a tiny New Mexico community just north of the Texas line and in the western shadows of the Guadalupe Mountains. The closest town for purchasing supplies was Van Horn, Texas, some seventy miles away.

Bill Earhart also moved away, his travels taking him to Pecos, Texas. He became embroiled in local hostilities and in 1896 was shot and killed in a Pecos bar.

Nettie Fry, once the betrothed of the murdered George McDonald, married Bill McNew, a friend of Oliver Lee. Over the years, Lee and McNew grew close, not so much as friends but as conspirators.

Of all of the participants in what was being referred to as the Tularosa Valley Feud, Oliver Lee eventually emerged the survivor. Always a hard and dedicated worker, Lee continued to make improvements on his ranches, at the same time acquiring more properties. In time, he became one of the most respected, and feared, citizens of the valley.

Lee remained outraged at the murder of his friend, George McDonald. He had sought to follow a course of prescribed legal action, and in so doing he located two of John Good's cowhands who could provide testimony that would identify the murderer and bring him to justice. Lee turned his witnesses' names, along with and explanation, over to the district attorney, but the two men were never called to testify.

This experience, along with others involving the legal system and law enforcement, soured Oliver Lee on the process. It was said that he possessed a sense of justice, but he remained thwarted and frustrated when he attempted to follow the established rules only to find that little could be accomplished.

6
ENTER ALBERT JENNINGS FOUNTAIN

The lawyers involved in the prosecution of Oliver Lee, Jim, Cooper, Perry Altman, Bill Kelham, and Tom Tucker during the Tularosa Valley feud included William R. Rynerson and a man named Wade. They were assisted by the noted Colonel Albert Jennings Fountain. The appearance of Fountain at this event marked the initial confrontation between him and Oliver Lee.

Fountain was born in New York City on October 3, 1838. His birth name was Albert Jennings, his father being Solomon Jennings, the captain of a merchant vessel. The maiden name of his mother, descended from French Huguenots and originally from Paris, was de la Fontaine.

Fountain was a product of New York public schools where he excelled as a student. He was provided a scholarship to Columbia College where, according to his own published accounts, he quickly established himself as a budding scholar. While at Columbia, Fountain, along with five fellow students, allegedly accompanied by a tutor, went on a tour around the world. While traveling in China, he adopted a version of his mother's name and was known thereafter as Albert Jennings Fountain. It is unclear whether or not Fountain ever graduated from Columbia, but it was obvious that he was well educated and experienced.

Fountain returned to the United States in 1859, disembarking in California. He secured a job as a newspaper reporter for the Sacramento *Union*. Like everything else he undertook, Fountain eclipsed his competition and established a name for himself, so much so that in 1860 he was sent to Central America to cover the Walker filibustering expedition. The Walker affair was related to the invasion of Nicaragua by an American named William Walker, who seized control of the country for a time.

Walker was a physician, lawyer, journalist and mercenary who conducted several expeditions into Latin America for the purpose of establishing English-speaking slave colonies under his control. According to Fountain's version of events, he was arrested and sentenced to be executed by a firing squad when he escaped and, disguised as a woman, boarded a steamer and returned to San Francisco.

Eager to explore and venture into new areas, Fountain studied law and was admitted to the California bar about the time of the outbreak of the Civil War. He immediately signed up for the California Column, a newly organized contingent of Union troops. The column was sent to New Mexico. By the time it arrived, Fountain had been promoted to corporal. On the way to New Mexico, according to Fountain, the column paused long enough to engage Apache chief Cochise in a two-day battle at Apache Pass in Arizona, a fight that pitted 110 soldiers against an estimated 1,200 Indians. Fountain's role in the conflict with the Apaches earned him sergeant stripes.

While the California Column saw no action with Confederates in New Mexico, it did engage in skirmishes with hostile Navajos and Apaches. The longer Fountain remained in New Mexico, the more he became attracted to the country, its vast landscapes, and what he regarded as its potential. He decided to stay. Shortly after his decision to become a resident, he married Mariana Perez de Ovante on October 27, 1862. She was fourteen-years-old and the sister of one of Fountain's fellow soldiers who invited him to his home for a visit. In time, Marianna would give him twelve children. On March 1, 1863, Fountain was promoted to second lieutenant.

Fountain received a discharge from the Union Army in 1865. He was not idle long. General Carleton talked him into reenlisting, assigned Fountain the rank of captain of cavalry, and gave him the responsibility of organizing a volunteer company of scouts and soldiers to engage the Apaches and Navajos. During a skirmish in Arizona, Fountain was wounded. He was sent to El Paso to recover, and while there, found himself embroiled in area politics.

W. W. Mills was the collector of customs assigned to El Paso and widely regarded as a local power. Mills has been described as "an intense, dynamic little man with a quick temper and a razor-sharp tongue." Fountain saw much to his liking in El Paso and was soon appointed an inspector of customs. He was Mills' chief assistant.

Fountain soon found himself among a cadre of unprincipled and unethical politicians and businessmen motivated primarily by ambition and greed. They included Louis Cardis, an Italian who controlled the Mexican vote, a large percentage of El Paso voters. There was also Father Antonio Borrajo, a Catholic priest in San Elizario, twenty-one miles downriver from El Paso. Borrajo was described as a "white-haired, thin-faced, terrible-tempered old man who was absolute master in his own province." These men, along with others, schemed to take over the salt deposits near the Guadalupe Mountains one hundred miles to the east. As this maneuvering was going on, Fountain decided he wanted to be elsewhere. He requested and was granted a leave of absence so he could join the forces of Benito Juarez in Mexico. Fountain organized an artillery unit, was awarded the rank of full colonel, and provided valuable assistance in the storming of Ciudad Chihuahua.

On returning to El Paso, Fountain became aware of a significant rift among the political elite. Mills' father-in-law, A. J. Hamilton, was running as the conservative Republican candidate for governor of Texas. His opposition came in the form of E. J. Davis. To Mills' disgust, Fountain supported Davis. Fountain also decided to run for a seat in the state senate. Davis won, and a short time later Mills was removed as collector of customs.

Mills was bitter. He began blaming Fountain for everything that was wrong in El Paso, if not the entire state of Texas. He scorned Fountain in articles and pamphlets, and even went as far as having him indicted in the United States District Court on eighteen separate counts. Fountain was finally brought into court in 1872 and cleared of all charges.

B. F. Williams was a lawyer who was close to Mills and counted on profiting from the acquisition of the vast salt deposits located just west of the Guadalupe and Delaware Mountains. He, as with so many of Mills' confederates, despised Fountain. Williams was drinking heavily in Ben Dowell's saloon in El Paso one afternoon when Fountain walked in. Loudly, Williams began insulting and condemning Fountain as well as District Judge Gaylord J. Clarke. In the embrace of alcohol, Williams pulled a derringer from his coat pocket and fired at Fountain, causing a minor flesh wound. Fountain stepped toward his attacker and was thrashing him with his cane when Williams fired again, striking Fountain a second time. Out of bullets, Williams fled to a nearby room and locked the door.

Fountain had had enough of Williams. Wounded and bleeding, he made his way to his home a few blocks away to retrieve his rifle. On the way he encountered Judge Clarke and explained what had occurred. Clarke immediately notified Captain French of the state police. Together, Clarke and French walked back to Ben Dowell's saloon to arrest Williams. The lawyer was still barricaded in the room and refused to come out. French notified him that he was under arrest. When Williams continued to refuse to open the door, French tried to break it down. Suddenly, Williams pulled the door open and rushed out of the room brandishing a shotgun. Raising it toward Clarke, he fired, killing the judge. Captain French fired his pistol at Williams. At the same time Fountain, who had just arrived, fired a shot from his rifle. Both bullets hit their target and Williams collapsed to the floor, dead.

As a result of his feud with Mills, Fountain had acquired a number of enemies. Now with his role in the killing of Williams, even though it was declared self-defense, he made even more. Fountain began receiving threats and was the subject of hostile discussion throughout El Paso. He ultimately decided the border town was not the place he needed to be. In 1875 when his term in the Texas legislature was over, he and his family moved to Mesilla, New Mexico. After settling into his new home, Fountain was once again involved in controversy.

After arriving in Mesilla, Fountain opened a law practice and soon became very successful. He leaned toward taking cases for the poor, the oppressed, the underdog, and many of his clients were Mexican citizens. Since Fountain spoke excellent Spanish, he communicated well and soon found great support in the Mexican community. According to author Sonnichsen, Fountain was "a...fighter...and he liked to defeat the buccaneers who came to New Mexico to grab land or leadership or public office." Fountain particularly despised cattle rustlers and swore to have them run down, arrested, and prosecuted at every turn. Time and again, Fountain regularly defeated such people. As a result, he became one of the best-loved men in the state. He also became one of the most hated.

In 1878, Apache chief Victorio and his renegade band raided up and down the Rio Grande Valley sacking churches and small communities, attacking travelers, and stealing livestock. Never one to shy away from a fight, Fountain was active in organizing a militia and defending communities and pursuing the predators. Similarly, gangs of toughs, rustlers, and robbers were busy throughout much of southern New Mexico. New Mexico Territorial Governor Sheldon made Fountain a major in a volunteer cavalry unit whose main responsibility was to counteract the outlaws. In no time at all, Fountain and his riders went after the notorious Kinney Gang in the town of Rincon. After one of its members was killed, the rest were captured save for one who fled to El Paso. From El Paso the outlaw sent threats to Fountain, stating that he would kill him if it were the last thing he did. Fountain had wearied of the blustering thug and went after him. He traveled to El Paso by train, located the man at a section of town called Concordia, and arrested him. On returning the outlaw back to Mesilla, he effected an escape. Jumping from the train at the Fillmore station, he took off running. Fountain fell in behind him in pursuit. When the outlaw was forty yards away, Fountain, according to his own testimony, raised his revolver, aimed, and shot him dead.

Following the incident, Fountain was harshly criticized by another newcomer to the area, Albert B. Fall. Fall claimed Fountain shot the prisoner, who was in handcuffs, in the back at close range. Fall ended his criticism by stating, "Now this is only one of many cases in which this man has done dirty work." Fountain and Fall would grow to become bitter enemies.

Fall's criticism did not go unnoticed by Fountain. It deterred him not one whit, for the colonel and his militia continued to pursue and arrest rustlers and ne'er-do-wells. A cattle rustling gang that operated around Hillsboro was broken up, and members of the so-called Farmington Gang that had a hideout in the Black Range near Silver City were either killed, arrested, or dispersed. The pursuit, arrest, and conviction of livestock rustlers took up a great deal of Fountain's time and attention throughout much of his life.

In a departure from his pursuit of outlaws, Fountain served as defense council for the outlaw Billy the Kid during his famous trial in Mesilla in 1881. His defense proved somewhat inadequate as the Kid was convicted of murdering a lawman and sentenced to hang. In 1886, Fountain accepted an appointment as Assistant United States District Attorney to assist in putting a halt to land frauds that were plaguing the Territory of New Mexico. In this office, he managed to acquire even more enemies.

As if being involved in politics and making decisions that often affected many in a negative manner wasn't enough, Fountain further enraged a contingent of New Mexico citizens when he co-founded and took on the position of editing a newspaper, the Mesilla *Independent.* Many of his columns came under the heading of "reminiscences" wherein he recalled aspects and adventures of his self-described exciting past and portrayed himself as the hero in many of them. Fountain was also "violently anti-Jesuit" and attacked the Catholic priesthood from time to time. This caused concern among his wife's family, all Catholics, as well as most of the Mexican community. With regard to politics, Fountain spared no one who opposed his philosophies. The Republican Fountain was staunchly anti-Democrat and made no bones about it.

Albert Jennings Fountain had a strong personality and at times could be intimidating. He possessed an abundance of courage, was goal-oriented, and stopped at nothing. He made a lot of enemies, men who despised him and everything he stood for. Author Sonnichsen wrote that "in New Mexico in those days it was necessary to have enemies, and it was a credit to a person to have the right ones."

Fountain could also be a useful citizen, and he was a more than competent lawyer. He loved giving speeches and wearing his military uniform in the courtroom. There is no doubt that he broke up cattle rustling gangs, but some of his critics insist he accomplished such things outside the law. It was rumored that Fountain often saw to the hanging of rustlers on being captured rather than arresting them and returning them for trial. These charges came often, but none were ever verified. Among ranchers and residents in the Tularosa Basin, Oliver Lee was suspected of being the most efficient and effective cattle rustler of them all, and it was via such tactics, they claimed, that he built up is impressive herd. Lee began to attract notice from Fountain and not much time would pass when they came face to face with one another.

In 1888, Fountain was approached by several influential New Mexico Republicans and asked to run for the Territorial Legislature. When he accepted the challenge the Democrats lost no time in attacking him, slinging mud, and reviving many of his negative experiences in Texas. Fountain loudly and often expressed contempt for his adversaries. When the Democrats met in September 1888, they nominated Albert Bacon Fall to run against him. The already bitter enemies were now pitted together in a political race, and it was about to get ugly. Standing on the sidelines and watching intently was Oliver Milton Lee.

7
ENTER ALBERT BACON FALL

During his career as a lawyer, newspaperman, and politician Albert Jennings Fountain accumulated an impressive roster of enemies. At times, it seemed as though he delighted in antagonizing those whose leanings and philosophies were the opposite of his. Throughout his life, Fountain had no greater adversaries than Oliver Lee and Albert Bacon Fall.

Fall was born in Frankfort, Kentucky, on November 26, 1861. His father was William Fall, who held the rank of captain in General Nathan Bedford Forrest's regiment of Confederate cavalry. After the war, the elder Fall became a teacher. Though he loved his position, Fall did not earn much money and the family was generally poor. Young Albert had few opportunities for an education and was forced to take a job in a cotton mill at the age of eleven in order to help support the family. Albert had his intentions set on becoming a preacher like his grandfather, but as he moved into his late teens he became attracted to the profession of law. He obtained law books and studied them at every opportunity. He landed a job as a school teacher which he pursued for two years. In the evenings following his meal, Fall would devote his attention to his studies. He obtained a position as a law clerk in the offices of Judge William Lindsley, who later went on to become a United States senator.

The Kentucky environment had a negative effect on Albert Fall's health, and he determined that a milder climate would be beneficial. He resigned his position at Lindsley's law firm and headed west, traveling through Arkansas and Oklahoma and finally arriving at Clarksville, Texas, sixty miles west of Texarkana. There he found work in a variety of fields: farming, ranch hand, clerking in a grocery store, and as a chuck-wagon cook. Tiring of the tedium of these jobs, he sought greater adventures, and by the time he turned twenty-one he was working in a mine near Nieves in the Mexican state of Zacatecas.

Needing to return to Clarksville to tidy up some business affairs, Fall decided to remain for a time. He found opportunities in real estate and insurance and opened an office to deal in both. During this time in Clarksville, Fall met Emma Morgan, the daughter of an important lawyer. She was eighteen, and though engaged to another, was impressed by Fall's charms. He began to court her; she was flattered and responsive, but reminded him of her commitment. Emma grew confused, and to secure some time to think over her dilemma, she traveled to Tennessee to remain for a time with relatives while she pondered her future.

Fall was determined to win Emma's hand. No sooner had she departed for Tennessee than he purchased a train ticket and arrived almost at the same time she did. Young and determined, Albert must have been quite persuasive, for the two were wed on May 8, 1881, in Woodville, Tennessee. Throughout the remainder of Fall's life and amid all of his triumphs and difficulties, Emma stood by his side, his greatest admirer and supporter.

Returning to Clarksville, Fall went back to work but made little money. In order to supplement his income, he opened a grocery store but saw little success with this enterprise. As the colder months of autumn set in, Fall returned to Mexico and the mining business. While there, he learned of the discovery of silver in New Mexico, particularly in Grant and Sierra Counties. He decided to return and try his luck. By May 1884, he was prospecting out of a camp he set up near the town of Kingston in the Black Range. While Fall did not make the fortune he anticipated, he received a valuable education relative to the business of mining and mining contracts.

While Fall was trying to harvest silver from the rock matrix of the Black Range, Emma was tending hearth and home back in Clarksville. Fall returned home only rarely, and after three years found himself the father of two children he hardly ever saw. Further, the work of keeping the home together and tending to two young ones had a deleterious effect on Emma's health. She was diagnosed with tuberculosis, and her doctor recommended a change of climate. On learning this, Fall was determined to relocate his family to the dry, clear air of New Mexico.

With little money and less hope of obtaining any, Fall moved his wife and children to Las Cruces. As he intended to find work somewhere, he was concerned about leaving Emma and the children alone. Luck was with them, for Emma's brother, Joe Morgan, agreed to travel to Las Cruces and provide help. While Fall looked for work, Joe took care of the children and tended the house while Emma rested.

Fall found work and settled into living in this new community. Fall never lacked confidence and ability, and as a result succeeded at various levels. In a short time in his new home, Fall, a keen observer, decided that politics was his short cut to wealth, power, and prestige. New Mexico was still a young territory and in need of laws and regulations. Fall decided that was the direction he wanted to go, to be involved in such things. This line of thinking led him to running for a seat in the House of the Territorial Legislature. Though young, new in the area, and relatively unknown, Fall, a Democrat, decided to oppose Albert Jennings Fountain, a Republican, in the contest. The year was 1888. Fall campaigned with great enthusiasm, but as it was his first contest of that nature, he was unskilled in the harsh reality of election politics, the under-the-table deals, the courting of power and influence, and the sometimes dirty fighting between candidates.

By the time the votes were counted, Fountain, to no one's surprise, won. Fall's ego made the loss difficult for him to accept. The Republicans were fairly well-entrenched in the area politics, and for the Democrats it was to a be a tough fight to make any headway at all. In spite of the odds against him, Fall agonized over his loss. He hated defeat, and the focus of his hatred was directed toward Fountain.

Though Fountain had won the election, it was by a margin of only forty-two votes out of 2,000 cast. Fountain went on to the Territorial Legislature and soon afterward was elected Speaker of the House. Fall watched from afar, already making plans to oppose Fountain at the next election. It was a fight he wanted, one that he felt he was ready for. Fall now worked harder than ever to secure his political foundation.

The fomenting battle between Fountain and Fall seemed inevitable, and couldn't have been scripted with any greater confrontational drama. Fountain was a Northerner, Fall a Southerner. Fountain was an established power, middle-aged, and had made a name for himself as a soldier, lawyer, politician, and newspaper columnist. His wife was Mexican and was well known and well thought of among the Spanish speaking block of voters in the region. Fountain's allies were others in power: the businessmen, the large ranchers, the moneyed.

Albert Fall, on the other hand, was attracted to the newcomers to the area, those many immigrants, many of them Texans such as Oliver Lee who, like him, were working hard trying to make a living in the region in spite of the numerous obstacles thrown up, the majority of them by backers of Albert J. Fountain. Fountain was convinced Fall lacked ethics and was deceitful, and did not hesitate to communicate his thoughts to others. Fall believed Fountain to be dishonest and a cheat who would stop at nothing to get elected.

In spite of their differences, Fountain and Fall had a number of things in common: Both had large egos, both were proud, and both were fearless. Fall wasted no time in preparing himself for the next election.

In March 1889, with help from his real estate partner, a man named Lowery, Fall undertook a campaign wherein he identified himself as a successful real estate, stock, and mine broker, thereby inserting him into the world of successful and established businessmen. In April, Fall was admitted to the New Mexico bar association. People began taking notice. Fall was approached and asked to think about running for sheriff in 1890. He declined, for his sights were set on a larger target.

Fall decided to oppose Fountain once again in the contest for the New Mexico Territorial Legislature. Fountain's Republicans surged forth with attacks aimed at Fall, calling him a "pygmy and a baby beside Col. Fountain...[a] would-be non-entity...absolutely worthless to anybody." Fall, anticipating a tough fight, retaliated and forged a campaign that won him a number of admirers. By the time it was all over, Fall had won, and Fountain, who had expected to walk away with the victory, came in an embarrassing third. The Republicans responded by claiming that Fall had provided free whiskey to the voters clear up to the day of the election. They also claimed that there were several dozen illegal votes. None of the claims were proven.

Fall felt he was gaining positive momentum. That, coupled with his natural brashness and confidence allowed him to feel as though he could not be stopped. While he was enjoying his victory, Fall continued to pursue his mining interests in the Sacramento and Organ Mountains, this time in partnership with his brother-in-law Joe Morgan. Such activity formed the basis for Fall's near lifetime in mining. Fall himself did little hard rock mining; he preferred instead to stake prospectors and purchase and sell mining claims.

It was around this time that Fall became interested in having his own newspaper. During his run for electoral office he witnessed the influence newspapers had on voters. The fact that his nemesis Fountain was active in penning columns and observations in newspapers did not escape Fall. Fall was convinced he could shape public opinion via columns of his own. In partnership with one or more family members, Fall founded the Las Cruces *Independent Democrat.* Fall's name appeared on the masthead as editor.

At the same time, Fall's law office saw an increase in activity as he was sought out more and more by the Texans and other newcomers to the Tularosa Basin for legal counsel. Many of the issues Fall dealt with had to do with water rights. One such case brought Fall into court to face Albert Jennings Fountain.

A rancher from the eastern slope of the Sacramento Mountains named W. A. Miley brought suit against James Gerard and a number of other ranchers for channeling water out of the river that he relied on for his cattle and crops. He petitioned that, since he was the first to settle in that area and make use of the water that he had priority. Gerald *et al* claimed that they had as much right to the water as did Miley.

Miley was represented by William R. Rynerson and his partner Edward Clements Wade. Fountain was called in to assist. All three men were closely tied to the big money enterprises in the Tularosa area and all were Republicans. Gerald *et al* were represented by Fall and his associate R. F. Young. For the first time, Fall and Fountain found themselves in the same courtroom on opposing sides. Fountain was described as being "at ease" in the courtroom, "switching from Spanish to English and back again, enjoying the sound of his big voice." It was noted that Fall was "intense and determined, watching for every joint in his foe's armor." Confrontations between Fountain and Fall would recur for the next two decades, with the animosity and hatred for one another growing with each occasion.

In 1889, an unscheduled meeting between Albert B. Fall and Oliver Lee would mark the onset of a strong relationship that would endure for the next several decades, with each man depending on the other for a variety of assistance and support.

Fall was in his law office one day when the door opened and a rugged looking, tanned, and poised man wearing a battered rancher hat stepped inside and introduced himself as Oliver Lee. Lee was aware of Fall's concern for the newcomers, and how ably he represented them in court. Lee perceived that Fall had the potential to become a valuable ally in his ongoing ranching concerns as well as his difficulties with the region's power brokers, all allies of Albert Jennings Fountain.

Author Sonnichsen described the meeting between Lee and Fall "the beginning of a grand alliance." Sonnichsen claimed the men had "become indispensable to each other...[and that] Fall was soon acting as the 'inside man' of the team—lawyer and strategist...[while] Lee was the 'outside man'—captain of the fighting force, a man of action." The two men developed a close friendship, closer than most brothers, and it lasted as long as they both lived. Lee would play a significant role in Fall's bid for re-election in 1892.

Fall campaigned aggressively this time around, rallying a growing number of Democrats around his platform in addition to recruiting many independents. Fall had organized an intelligent and competent campaign staff who traveled around the region soliciting voters. Seeing the results of Fall's successful bid, the Republicans grew nervous. Several of the leaders of the party decided it was time for "extreme measures." They summoned the state militia to monitor the polling places. Fall was convinced that this measure was to have the effect of intimidating honest voters and controlling the election. After raging about the situation for a day, Fall arrived at a solution. He would enlist his new friend Oliver Lee and his force of cowhands.

After mobilizing his fighting men, Lee led them on a ride into Las Cruces during the night before the election. They arrived and were in place before the Republican leadership had any notion of what was transpiring.

The voting boxes had been set up at the Masonic Temple across the street from Lohman's store. The store was a one-story adobe structure with a flat roof and a parapet. Lohman, though a Republican, was a good friend of Fall's and, after receiving a request, provided his store for the setting of what was to follow.

When Lee and his men arrived, they tied their horses behind the store, checked their rifles and revolvers, and climbed to the roof and stationed themselves behind the parapet where they had a wide angle view of the street. Lohman had extra weapons and ammunition sent to the roof, which overlooked a perfect field of fire.

Shortly after dawn, a contingent of New Mexico Territorial militiamen under the command of W. H. H. Llewellyn and Captain Thomas Brannigan appeared at one end of the street. Led by the two officers, the armed command marched toward the polling place where they were to take up positions. As they neared the Masonic Temple, Las Cruces citizens, sensing trouble, dispersed and took shelter. Albert Fall stepped from Lohman's store out into the center of the street facing the militia and raised his arms as a signal for them to halt. Surprised and confused, Llewellyn and company reined up. Before Llewellyn could say anything, according to author William A. Keleher, Fall said, "Llewellyn, get the hell out of here with that damned militia or I will have you all killed." As he stated his command, he pointed toward the rooftop of Lohman's store where Oliver Lee and his men had rifles pointed at the soldiers. It took Llewellyn and Brannigan mere seconds to determine that they were out-armed and likely outnumbered. Without a word, they turned the militiamen around and led them back to their camp.

When the votes were counted, Fall had been victorious once again. Charges were hurled that fraud had been committed, and that Fall had recruited ineligible voters. None of the charges were proven. Fall traveled once again to the capital at Santa Fe where he worked hard and won the respect of members of both parties. He was described as "pugnacious yet courteous." An editorial in the Santa Fe *New Mexican* referred to Fall as "a hard and at times a bitter fighter but he has the courtesy of a brave man. His future is bright...."

In addition to serving the Territorial Legislature, Fall was named judge of the Third Judicial District, which was composed of Doña Ana, Grant, and Sierra Counties. In the meantime, Fountain fumed and sputtered, and waited for his next chance to go after Fall.

Albert B. Fall

from Coleman. Stepping into the center of the street blocking the path and raised his arms as a signal for them to halt. Surprised and confused, Llewellyn and Coleman [illegible]. Llewellyn [illegible] not trying to capture Williams & Ketchum," [illegible] said. "Llewellyn, get the hell out of here with [illegible], or I will have you all killed." [illegible] his companion, he [illegible] to read the [illegible] Coleman [illegible] and [illegible] determined that they were [illegible] Without a word, they [illegible] back to [illegible].

When the [illegible] was continued, Fall and the defendants once again [illegible] were [illegible] had been committed, and that Fall had [illegible]. None of the charges were proven. Fall traveled once again to the capital at Santa Fe, where he worked hard and won the respect of members of both parties. He was described as [illegible].

In addition to serving as Territorial Legislator, Fall was named judge of the Third Judicial District, which was composed of Doña Ana, Grant, and Sierra Counties, in the meantime. [illegible] immediately [illegible] and [illegible] charges to prosecute Fall.

Albert B. Fall

8
DROUGHT AND TROUBLE

For years, the Tularosa Basin provided a livelihood for dozens of ranchers and farmers who found a land of relatively abundant rainfall and clear flowing streams much to their liking. The graze for cattle seemed endless, and the harvests of everything from family gardens to commercial produce farms was impressive. The corn grew twelve feet high and watermelons weighed forty pounds. Cattle were fat and contented.

So appealing was the commercial success and associated progress in the Tularosa Basin that people flocked in from other parts of the Southwest. Several families with hopes of making a good living at farming moved into and settled onto open lands. Area boosters bragged that the Tularosa Basin was the garden spot of the universe. To add to the momentum of immigration, a rumor surfaced that a line for the El Paso and White Oaks Railroad would be constructed through the area. The excitement brought in more optimists and men seeking business opportunities. The population of Tularosa doubled in four weeks during the spring of 1888. Difficulties, however, loomed on the horizon.

Beginning in the summer of 1889, the worst drought in the history of the region struck the Tularosa Basin. Ranchers and farmers struggled but held on in the hope that the disaster would soon be over, but it was not to be. By the summer of 1890, streams and ponds had dried up and hundreds of cattle died from lack of water. Dead animals clogged the drying-up water holes. The rivers and creeks were flush with maggots from rotting cattle carcasses.

By this time several of the small farmers were forced to give up and move away. Many of those that remained resorted to stealing cattle for meat. Hopes for a better life were dashed, promises of growing and progressive communities seemed a distant dream. The disaster was widespread and few were spared. "Hard times," wrote Sonnichsen, "naturally gave an extra nudge to lawlessness which was already tormenting the region." Several disagreements over water rights had resulted in shootings. Rustling was on the increase, brands were altered, and normally decent and honest men stooped to levels never before thought of in order to survive.

The year 1893 saw the beginning of some relief from the drought, but by this time a great deal of damage had been done, not only to the integrity of the ranching and farming operations, but to relationships between neighbors. A line had been drawn and sides taken. One side consisted of the small ranchers and farmers, many of whom arrived years earlier from Texas. There included Oliver Lee, Perry Altman, and their friends and family. The opposite side was made up of the large ranchers, most of whom rode the wave of earlier settlement and who resented the Texas newcomers. They also resented most of the politicians in power and sought to back their own choices for office.

Oliver Lee was the most vocal of the Texas newcomers. He claimed that the larger cattle companies were trying to run the smaller operators like him out of business by buying up all of the available ranch land. While some of the tactics of the larger ranchers ranged from being suspicious to downright illegal, they had the politicians and law enforcement officials on their side. In turn, they accused the small operators of rustling, intimidation, and threats. They identified Oliver Milton Lee as the leader of the Texans and other small ranchers as the cause of most of their troubles.

There is no doubt that cattle rustling took place, or that it was, in fact, a common practice in the Tularosa Basin. Charges and counter charges were filed often in the courts relative to rustling on both sides of the squabble. Strays and mavericks were often incorporated into a rancher's herd. If the strays were branded, they were normally set aside for butchering, thus removing the evidence of stolen calves. It was said that most of the ranchers in this area seldom ate their own beef.

All ranchers kept a lookout for unclaimed or motherless calves, the so-called mavericks. As soon as possible, the maverick would be marked with the brand of the man who found it. It was said that many a herd got its start from acquiring mavericks.

Mavericking proved to be a source of trouble for many of the ranchers, but it was not the only one. Another practice that generated difficulties among the cattlemen was the practice of "accommodation branding." During a group roundup, a rancher or cowhand who came across a calf following a cow belonging to a neighbor was expected to brand it with the owner's brand. This practice, which operated on the honor system, was often violated.

Lee continued to operate his ranch as before, although somewhat limited as a result of the drought. Continuing to assist him as ranch hands were Cherokee Bill and Tom Tucker. To this core of workers he hired Bill McNew and Jim Gilliland.

Like so many others in the Tularosa Basin, McNew had arrived from Texas. He was described as having ice-blue eyes and was perceived to be a tough character. McNew married Nettie Fry a short time after the dearth of her betrothed, George McDonald. As a result, McNew became part of the Lee clan.

Jim Gilliland came from Brownwood, Texas, and though younger than McNew, brought a wealth of experience working with livestock. Gilliland has been characterized as tall, lanky, iron-nerved, and generally agreeable when he wasn't drinking. He fought often and backed down from no man.

When the Texans found themselves in court against the large operators, their attorney was Albert B. Fall. Siding with the Texans made Fall numerous enemies. Along with Lee, most of the small ranchers in the basin and along the foothills of the Sacramento Mountains looked upon Fall as one of their leaders and one of their own, one capable of manipulating the law in favor of his clients.

A major confrontation between the Texans and the big ranchers occurred in 1894. There was abundant rain that year, enough to fill what ranchers in that area call "wet weather lakes." These were simply low areas that filled up with runoff after heavy rains and served as sources of water for the cattle. One such wet weather lake was located at the northern part of the Jicarilla Mountains near Cox's Well. The small ranchers in the area, sometimes desperate for a source of water, took advantage of it.

On hearing of this source of important water, a man named Garst, who was the manager of one of the large ranches, decided to herd 5,000 head of cattle to the lake. Accompanying this massive cattle herd was another of 4,000 goats. On learning of this, Oliver Lee gathered his ranch hands, along with several neighbors, and turned the Garst-led herd away from the lake. Lee sent word to Garst to keep his stock off of the part of the range that was used by the small ranchers. Garst ignored the warning.

From time to time, one or more of Garst's cowhands would report that some of their cattle would be missing. The reports increased, and as a result Garst had the herd moved farther from the reach of the rustlers, whom he assumed were the Texans. The incident added to the tension between the two groups.

During the ensuing months, the rustling continued. In particular, the big corporate ranchers were hurt the worst, and it would be easy to jump to the conclusion that the herds of many of the small ranchers were kept up as a result of stock being added from the larger ranchers. In spite of this, some of the small ranchers were also subjected to rustling, and one who suffered the worst was Oliver Lee.

A significant number of cattle were discovered missing from one of Lee's herds. Studying the tracks, he determined that the animals had been rounded up and herded away to the south toward Texas. He summoned Bill McNew and the two went in pursuit. Lee trailed the herd to a location near the Hueco Mountains thirty miles east of El Paso. The Hueco Mountains were represented by a scattering of large granite outcrops. Within the range were several springs, and the area had long been a popular spot for Apaches, Comanches, and other tribes. The rock basins where the water gathered were referred to as "tanks," and Hueco Tanks became a favorite camping and recreational location for El Pasoans. (Today it is known as Hueco Tanks State Park and Historic Site).

When Lee and McNew arrived at the Hueco Mountains, they encountered George Gaither who was camping there with his son. The two had planned a few days of deer hunting. Lee asked Gaither if he had seen a herd of cattle. When Gaither replied in the negative, Lee said he would need to backtrack in order to pick up the trail again. Noticing Gaither's .44 caliber rifle, Lee asked if he could borrow it. When Gaither hesitated, Lee said that when he caught up with his stolen cattle herd there might be some fighting. Gaither handed over the rifle. The two men talked some more and Lee learned that Gaither owned and operated a butcher shop in El Paso. Lee told him that he would have the rifle returned to his place of business.

Lee and McNew turned and headed back toward the north where they picked up the trail of the herd and followed it northwestward. The two men rode at a steady trot in hope of catching up to the herd soon. Near the tiny railroad station at Newman, some twenty miles northeast of El Paso, the tracks of the herd turned south. Lee presumed the rustlers intended to take the stolen cattle into Mexico. The Rio Grande border was twenty miles away. Lee and McNew increased their pace and not too much time passed before they spotted the herd ahead of them. It consisted not only of some of Lee's cattle but those of other small ranchers. The herd was tended by only two cow hands who, when they spotted the pursuit, stopped to face the oncoming strangers.

When Lee and McNew got close enough, they recognized the rustlers—Matt Coffelt and Charley Rhodius from Crow Flats were known to Lee. Neither of them had the reputation of rustlers. After exchanging a few words, Lee rode into the herd with the intention of cutting out his cows. As he was doing so, and while his back was to him, Rhodius fired a shot at Lee. Manifesting utmost cool, Lee turned in his saddle and fired back, killing Rhodius. Coffelt went for his own weapon and was killed a moment later.

Leaving McNew with the herd, Lee rode into El Paso to report the incident. This done, he telegraphed Albert Fall in Las Cruces and requested he come to El Paso to take care of any problems associated with the incident. With Fall running interference, the case was cleared up in a short time and Lee was not indicted. True to his word, after settling the legalities in town, Lee carried the .44 caliber rifle to Gaither's butcher shop as he had promised.

9
LEE'S LETTER TO PAT GARRETT

By 1892 most citizens of the American Southwest, as well as other parts of the country, were familiar with the name Pat Garrett. Garrett rose to fame on the back of his claim that he shot and killed the notorious outlaw, Billy the Kid. Garrett's claim has long been in question. Witnesses at the scene disputed it at various times, and subsequent investigations into the shooting employing forensic techniques have yielded the information that Garrett lied, that he shot the wrong man, and that Billy the Kid went on to live a long but not necessarily happy life. (See *Billy the Kid: Beyond the Grave,* W. C. Jameson, and *Billy the Kid: Investigating History's Mysteries,* W. C. Jameson.)

Oliver Lee was aware of who Pat Garrett was, as well as his reputation. By this time, Lee had not encountered Garrett, but would on several occasions in the future, none of them pleasant. Their final encounter led to the assassination of the arrogant and egotistical lawman. During the month of June 1892, an incident occurred at Lee's ranch that compelled him to write a letter to Garrett.

June 21, 1892

Pat Garrett
c/o Doña Ana County Sheriff's Office
Las Cruces, New Mexico

Dear Sheriff Garrett,

It is common knowledge in these parts that you are credited with killing the outlaw known as Billy the Kid back in '81.

This last week I had a most unusual experience I thought you might be interested in. One warm evening I was sitting on the porch of my ranch about half way between Lincoln and El Paso in Otero county. As I sat there, a strange man rode up. He appeared to be in his late twenties or early thirties and carried his gun like he knew how to use it. We exchanged salutations and I invited him to stay and chat a while. We sat on the porch and watched tumbleweeds blow by in the breeze and talked about old times. This man talked at some length about the Lincoln County War and his part in it. He seemed to have no use for lawman (sic)—except for you. After a while the man got back on his horse and rode away. I had not gotten the man's name and was a bit caught aback when, just before riding off, he told me his name was Billy Bonny (sic). I remember hearing somewhere that Billy the Kid was sometimes known as William Bonny (sic) and that it was rumored that he was in fact still alive. I don't know who this man was for sure, but I thought you would like to know of this unusual turn of events.

Your Friend,

Oliver Lee
Circle Cross Ranch
Otero County, New Mexico

It is not known whether or not Garrett replied to the letter from Lee. The letter did serve the purpose of informing Garrett that Lee had doubts regarding his credibility and veracity.

10
ENTER TODD BAILEY

Around the year 1890, a young man only eleven years old arrived at the Lee ranch. He was tired, worn, and haggard, having traveled hundreds of miles on foot. He was the grandson of Mary Lee and a nephew to Oliver. His name was Charles Lewis Bailey, but he had always been called Todd. His coming years of long association with Oliver Lee was to have a profound influence and effect on both men, one which led to the deaths of a number of prominent historical figures.

Charles Lewis Bailey was born on July 12, 1879, in Buffalo Gap, Texas, to parents Rutha and John Wesley Bailey. Rutha's maiden name was Altman, and she was the older half-sister to Oliver Lee. A younger sister gave the boy the name "Todd," by which he was called for the rest of his life.

When Todd was two years old, his older brother, named Oliver after Oliver Lee, was killed in wagon accident. He was only seven years old. Two years later, Todd's mother died, leaving the boy and his sister, Mamie, to be raised by their father. Shortly after moving the family to Commerce, Texas, one account has John Wesley Bailey dying from a heart attack and the children placed into the care of a neighbor. According to Bailey descendants, however, John simply dropped the children off at the home of their uncle Charlie Hass and his wife and rode away. Todd was not yet six years old.

Life in the Hass household was difficult and unpleasant. The uncle worked the children from dawn to dusk and treated them poorly, often whipping them for lagging in their chores. Todd grew to despise his uncle, but options were few for an orphan. From New Mexico, Mary Lee learned that her grandchildren were being treated harshly by their guardians, so she sent son Oliver to Commerce to retrieve them and bring them to the

New Mexico ranch. Oliver made the journey to Commerce, but succeeded in returning with only one child—Todd's sister Mamie. The reason for not securing both of the children was never learned.

On July 6, 1890, six years after depositing his children on the doorstep of Charlie Hass, Todd's father, John Wesley Bailey, rode up to the Commerce home. He unsaddled his horse, walked over to the front porch without saying a word to anyone, threw the saddle to the ground, lay down using the saddle for a pillow, and died.

One afternoon when Charlie Hass thought young Todd was not working hard enough, he lashed him with a horsewhip, opening cuts on the boy's face and chest. Todd fell against a wagon wheel where he was pinned, unable to flee as Hass continued to whip him. Todd tried to roll away and wound up on top of a pitchfork as the whip laced across his back. He was certain his uncle was trying to kill him.

From the ground, Todd seized the pitchfork and thrust it upward, hard, and plunged it into his uncle's stomach and deep into the rib cage. Hass fell to the ground, blood pouring out of his wound and puddling on the hay-covered sod. Through his tears, Todd Bailey watched his hated uncle writhing on the ground, moaning in pain. Todd turned and ran, pausing at a shallow creek some distance away long enough to ponder what he had done. He realized he could never go back, so he continued running. Todd Bailey was ten years old.

Amazingly, Todd made his way on foot to Abilene, Texas, a distance of 245 miles, and then to Buffalo Gap, another fifteen miles to the southwest. There, he hoped to find some Altman and Lee relatives. On arriving, he learned that they had all moved to New Mexico. Somehow, the youngster traveled by foot and hitched rides across seven hundred additional miles of arid West Texas and New Mexico landscape before arriving at the Lee ranch, nearly dead from starvation. There, he was reunited with his sister Mamie, and from that point on the two were raised by their grandmother Mary Lee.

As he grew up on the Lee ranch, Todd learned important livestock and riding skills from his uncle, Oliver Lee. Todd grew to become one of the ranch's most competent and dependable hands. In addition to teaching Todd ranching skills and horsemanship, Lee provided instruction on the care and use of rifles and revolvers. In time, Todd became as proficient a marksman as his uncle. This skill would be called into play on several occasions years later.

When Todd Bailey was in his early teens, Lee felt he was old enough to handle the responsibility of working as an agent for the ranch selling horses. Todd accepted the job with enthusiasm, and strove to please and impress his uncle. There was never a ranch hand more devoted and loyal to Oliver Lee than Todd Bailey. As time passed, Lee and a handful of his ranch hands introduced Todd to butchering skills, and the young man became adept at slaughtering, dressing, carving, and packing beef, lamb, and goats. For a time, Oliver Lee held a contract with the railroad to supply meat for the workers. The butchering operation took place in Carrizozo, a location of intense railroad construction activity. Later, Lee opened a butcher shop in Alamogordo.

Todd Bailey owed much to his uncle and would do anything for him. This commitment had a profound influence on history.

Todd Bailey went to his grave convinced that he had killed his uncle Charlie Hass. Though badly wounded when he was impaled by the pitchfork wielded by Todd, Hass recovered. Years later he moved to Victoria, Texas, where he lived out the rest of his life.

11
GET OLIVER LEE

As lines were being drawn between the two major ranching factions in the Tularosa Basin, animosity grew and suspicion crept into everyday affairs. In 1894 an event occurred that was to widen the rift and exacerbate the situation.

A man named C. F. Hilton arrived in the Tularosa Basin and homesteaded on the headwaters of the Sacramento River. (Many years later this location was to become the headquarters for the Circle Cross Ranch that was eventually managed by Oliver Lee.) Hilton formed a partnership with an El Paso druggist named W. A. Irvin. Irvin, in turn, had business dealings with ranchers Frank Garst and Andrew McDonald in an extensive land and cattle operation in the Tularosa Basin. The men formed a corporation, the objective of which was to purchase land in the region on which the smaller landowners from Texas had settled and were developing ranches, farms, and orchards. Hilton was named manager of the corporation.

With a crew of workers, Hilton cut a number of trees to be used as fence rails. He had the rails piled up and intended to return with a wagon to haul them to a designated location. A neighboring rancher, James Smith, claimed the rails were cut from his property and warned Hilton not to take them. Hilton ignored the claim and on February 18, 1894, he, along with three ranch hands—W. C. Babers, Jud McNash, and a man named McSmith—went to retrieve the rails. As they were loading them into a wagon, Smith arrived on horseback. He was accompanied by Silas Chatfield, his father-in-law, two of Chatfield's sons, and a ranch hand named York.

Smith and company pulled guns on Hilton and his men, none of whom were armed save for Hilton, who had a rifle in his saddle scabbard. Smith spurred his horse over to where Hilton sat astride his own and informed him he was going to kill him. Without another word, Smith shot Hilton, the impact knocking him from his horse. Moaning in pain, Hilton staggered to his feet and made an attempt to run away. Smith shot him again, and once more Hilton fell to the ground. As he writhed in agony, Smith rode close and placed yet another bullet into the head of his adversary, making certain he was dead.

On learning of the incident, Hilton's partner, W. A. Irvin, rode into Las Cruces to report the murder and to insist Smith be arrested. Smith remained elusive to the authorities for several days as he hid out in the nearby mountains. Eventually, however, he was located, arrested, and indicted. Smith chose Albert B. Fall as his defense attorney. Fall did a masterful job and Smith was acquitted. Newspaper writer John P. Meadows stated that, "There seemed to be plenty of money around [and] character witnesses for Hilton were never called."

The acquittal of James Smith was a bitter pill for the corporate ranchers to swallow and they lost no time in laying plans. Twenty-one of them gathered in Las Cruces to discuss what their priorities needed to be. Among them was to put an end to the cattle rustling they claimed was being conducted by the Texas newcomers to the basin. Before the meeting was adjourned, the cattlemen had formed the Southeastern New Mexico Livestock Association. Colonel Albert Jennings Fountain was appointed as the association's attorney. On learning of the new organization, Oliver Lee, who was suspected by most of them as a major cattle rustler, was somehow allowed to join.

Employing whatever means necessary and available, the association went after rustlers hard and fast. Once arrested and hauled into court, Fountain made certain they were punished for their crimes; at least twenty of the rustlers he prosecuted were given prison terms. Fountain was gaining a reputation as a man intent on prosecuting any and all cattle rustlers.

Rustling, however, continued. As it turned out, the twenty men Fountain sent to the penitentiary were for the most part small time operators, desperate men trying to scratch out a living and feed their families. The bigger targets remained elusive, but association members such as Irvin and McDonald were determined to go after the Texans. Bringing them into court, however, proved difficult, and it was largely associated with politics.

How the law was enforced in the Tularosa Basin depended to a significant degree on who was doing the enforcing and who was in political control. In the end, important legal matters went through the sheriff and the district attorney. Sonnichsen wrote that legal decisions "hinged partly on which side had won in the last election," and that the "game of politics meant life or death, freedom or jail to many people, and they played it with no holds barred."

As the Southeastern New Mexico Livestock Association swung into high gear, it was the Democrats who were in control of things. Albert Fall, a leading Democrat who was also the District Judge, was responsible for making the decisions, and the Republicans, including the corporate ranchers, were the real and potential losers.

Fall kept himself apprised of the plots and plans of the Republicans as much as possible. He found it useful to be aware of what the opposition was planning. To that end, he enlisted a number of friendly supporters who were to pay close attention to what was going on in the area and report back to him. One of his allies was Albert Ellis, a Las Cruces barber. In a town like Las Cruces, it was usually the barber who knew most of what was transpiring. As the campaign of 1894 approached, Fall went about his affairs with the confidence of knowing he had a leg up on the opposition.

The Republicans were growing desperate. They felt that if progress as they saw it was to happen in the Tularosa Basin, they needed to win the next election. Their energy and enthusiasm did not go unnoticed by the Democrats, who redoubled their own efforts, not all of them legal. When the messenger transporting the ballot box from Tularosa to Las Cruces for counting was traveling through San Augustin Pass, he was met by a group of men who took it away from him and burned the contents. Tularosa had been expected to vote almost entirely Republican.

The Republicans filed in court to have the election invalidated. They proved that the ballots in the box from Tularosa were Republican and that if they had not been destroyed they would have won. Albert Jennings Fountain represented the Republican contingent, and he found himself in court facing his nemesis, Albert B. Fall.

The courtroom was packed and Fountain, who always played well to a large crowd, was eloquent, confident. Fall, who had learned a lot over the years, defended his side "with fury and passion," objecting to nearly everything the opposition said. The key argument focused on the office of sheriff. The Republicans desperately wanted their man in office in order to aggressively pursue and arrest the cattle rustlers. They feared that the winner, Democrat Guadalupe Ascarate, would thwart this effort with postponements and delays. Ascarate, who was regarded as an inept lawman, was otherwise well thought of in the community, his one failing being, in the eyes of the Republicans, was that he was a tool of Albert Fall.

During Ascarate's earlier term as sheriff, he responded to a suggestion by Fall that he organize a squad of deputies to assist in enforcing the law. The deputies appointed were Oliver Lee, Bill McNew, and Fall's brother-in-law Joe Morgan. This stunned and outraged the Republicans, for in their minds the deputies that were appointed were the very ones they suspected of stealing their cattle.

Oliver Lee and company went out of their way to embarrass Fountain's men. One of their targets was Ben Williams, a former constable who was known to be doing undercover work for the Southeastern New Mexico Livestock Association. Lee humiliated Williams by confiscating his guns in Las Cruces. As a deputy, Lee had the legal right to bear arms, Williams did not. The humiliations piled up and did not go unnoticed by the cattle barons.

The Republicans did not wish to see such policies continued, and they could only be eliminated by removing Ascarate from office and proving that his opponent, Numa Reymond, had won. They succeeded in having the case placed on the docket of the District Court for a final determination. There it remained, however, for Albert Fall affected one delay after another, and Sheriff Ascarate remained in office to run the county's department as Fall determined it should be run.

In the meantime, Fountain continued to pursue, arrest, and convict small time cattle thieves, but the larger targets managed to elude him. Keeping an eye on Fountain's activities, the Texans, with Oliver Lee as their acknowledged leader, were convinced that Fountain was trying hard to close in on them to drive them out of business, to send them to jail. A number of the Texans—their identities were never a matter of record—had decided that Albert Jennings Fountain should be eliminated.

This conspiracy to kill Fountain never unfolded, and would have remained lost to history were it not for the testimony provided by a man Fountain had sent to prison for ten years for cattle rustling. Eli Miller, nicknamed Slick, agreed to meet with Pinkerton detectives in 1896 wherein he revealed the plot. Miller often went by the alias Jim Rose. His livestock rustling partners included Lee Williams, Abram Miller, Doc Evans, and Ed Brown.

Miller related that in 1894, eight of the Texans and a few other smaller ranchers concluded that it would be difficult to carry on their operations as long as Fountain and others continued to interfere. Miller knew the Texans well and listened to their schemes. He said their plan was to murder Fountain and corporate rancher W. C. McDonald, whose power and influence, they were convinced, heavily influenced Fountain's agenda. The killing was to be done by a man identified only as Powder Bill.

Miller was enlisted to participate in the killings. He claimed he was offered $500 and two horses. He opted not to be involved. According to Miller, the coalition upped the ante to $2,000, but he still refused.

Miller related the essentials of the plot to kill Fountain. At first, a location somewhere along the road from Las Cruces to Socorro was to be selected, but later abandoned when a more ideal one was determined—a remote section of road that wound through the White Sands. It was agreed that once Fountain was killed, his body was to be transported into the San Andres Mountains and thrown off a high ridge to lodge on a lower projection. In the San Andres, there was little grazing of cattle or any other livestock at the time, and the area was seldom visited save for an occasional deer hunter. Following the killing, those involved were to disperse and depart in different directions and obliterate their tracks. Two of the accomplices were to return to their ranches and herd their cattle across their tracks. According to the subsequent Pinkerton report, the plot could not be carried out because of the pending arrest of the leader and the departure of two other plotters who decided to leave the area. Under questioning by the Pinkerton agent, Miller revealed the names of those involved. They included Oliver Lee, Bill McNew, and Bill Carr. Miller also stated that the man in charge of the plot was Ed Brown.

Several of the Texas cattlemen were coming to regret that Fountain was not dispatched. By the close of 1894, it was clear that the Southeastern New Mexico Livestock Association was intent on arresting Oliver Lee, based on undercover work performed by Ben Williams. The Texas Rangers were brought into the case, since a significant percentage of the rustling attributed to Lee was taking place not only in New Mexico but across the state line in Texas. The cattle barons remained focused on one objective—get Oliver Lee.

Representatives of the Texas Rangers went to the El Paso County grand jury and obtained six indictments against Oliver Lee and Bill McNew—four for theft of cattle and two for brand alterations. The stock allegedly stolen by Lee and McNew belonged to the cattle company owned by Andrew McDonald, W. A. Irvin, and Frank Garst.

For reasons never explained, the case was never processed. A year passed before Lee and McNew even learned that they were to be indicted. As the stalling continued, McDonald and his company, tired of wasting time, brought in a cattle detective named Les Dow.

Dow was a Texan who had once served as a deputy sheriff in Chaves County, New Mexico. When he was summoned by McDonald, Dow was serving as a deputy U. S. marshal for the Texas-New Mexico Sanitary Association, his assignment to police the cattle industry on both sides of the Texas-New Mexico border. In this position, Dow learned that some cattle with altered brands could be found in a herd grazing in the foothills of the Sacramento Mountains. The herd was owned by Oliver Lee and Bill McNew.

Dow traveled to the region and kept a low profile until the group roundup was undertaken. During the cut, cattle and calves in the large herd were separated and turned over to their owners. At that point, Dow rode into the camp. As the various owners were claiming their stock, Dow located one of the steers that had been described to him. After examining the hide, he determined that the brand looked suspicious. Oliver Lee was not at the roundup, but Bill McNew was, and he was promptly arrested and handcuffed to a nearby wagon.

With assistance from the roundup cook, Dow skinned the animal and examined the hide. The brand had clearly been altered. Taking the hide and his prisoner, Dow traveled the nearly one hundred miles to Lincoln. McNew insisted they stop at Lee's ranch on the way but Dow refused. At Lincoln, McNew was handed over to the sheriff and the hide was presented to the grand jury, which happened to be in session at the time.

The cowhide was spread out on the courtroom floor. Carefully, Dow explained brand altering and pointed out the evidence showing that this hide was been tampered with. Following Dow's demonstration, the grand jury brought in indictments for "larceny of cattle" and "defacing brands" against Oliver Lee and Bill McNew. McNew was in custody. Now, it was time to get Oliver Lee.

12
WATER

Water has long been a precious commodity in southeastern New Mexico. Ranches and farms succeeded or failed based on its availability, and violent arguments raged over who had the rights to certain water sources—streams, ponds, or springs. One of the most dependable sources of water during the 1890s was a spring-fed stream that flowed out of Dog Canyon in the Sacramento Mountains. The water was clear, cool, and plentiful.

The source of the water was on a piece of land occupied by a man named Francois Jean Rochas. He liked to be called Frank, but the locals nicknamed him Frenchy. Frenchy was born in France in 1843 and migrated to America, arriving in southeastern New Mexico sometime in the mid-1880s when he was in his forties. His parents and siblings voiced disapproval of his leaving the family and his homeland, but Frenchy, who seemed to possess a keen sense of adventure and a desire to experience life beyond France, in turn disapproved of his family's condemnation of his pursuits. It had also been mentioned that his health caused him to seek milder climes such as could be found in the American Southwest.

Frenchy loved solitude, and he reveled in the peace and contentment he found in his isolated home near the mouth of Dog Canyon. He visited towns—Tularosa, Las Cruces, and Alamogordo—from time to time for supplies and provisions, but kept company with few. While he was generally regarded as friendly, he had only a handful of friends of his own choosing, preferring instead a solitary life. It was often mentioned in the area that Frenchy had the best water in the entire Tularosa Basin, and for that reason he was the envy of many. Those who knew him encouraged him to file a claim on his land in order to forestall any potential difficulties, but Frenchy could not be bothered with such formalities. With the good and abundant water at his disposal, Frenchy planted an extensive orchard—apple, peach, cherry, and pear—and developed a productive garden. He constructed a rock house, corrals, a long stretch of stone wall, and maintained the trail that led to the mouth of the canyon and out onto the flats. He also ran a herd of five hundred head of cattle.

A short distance to the south and not far from the mouth of Dog Canyon and Frenchy's residence was the ranch of Oliver Lee. From his perch high in the foothills near the canyon entrance, Frenchy watched as the area was being settled, the Lee ranch expanded, and the herds increased. It seemed to Frenchy that the newcomers—Texans—could never seem to acquire enough grass and water, and that the quest for such often led to fighting and occasionally violence. He was aware that the newcomers coveted his water. Down below in the foothills of the Sacramento Mountains, Oliver Lee occasionally cast covetous glances up the canyon toward Frenchy's spring. In 1893, Lee and his ranch hands excavated a mile-and-a-half-long ditch which diverted the downstream water from Frenchy's creek onto his pasture.

Occasionally cattle from Frenchy's neighbors' herds would wander up into Dog Canyon. Frenchy invariably herded them back down the trail toward the appropriate ranch. During group roundups, Frenchy learned to keep a wary eye out for neighbors he suspected of stealing his livestock.

Oliver Lee appeared to resent the Frenchman, accused him of stealing his cattle, and threatened him. Among the crowd that Lee ran with, it was often stated that eventually someone was going to put an end to the Frenchman.

During the drought years, ranchers' cattle were dying of thirst by the hundreds. Not so Frenchy's, who appeared to have all of the water they needed. When others were striving to just get by, Frenchy sold most of his herd for $3,400, and amount regarded as a fortune at the time. Nothing breeds contempt like success among some, and Frenchy's hard work and ultimate rewards irked many. From time to time Frenchy received warnings and threats to leave, but he ignored them.

Frenchy was reminded time and again that he never did file a claim on his place and never proved up on his water. In essence, he had no legal title to the Dog Canyon property.

During the early autumn of 1876, a rifleman, firing from the rocks above Frenchy's cabin, struck the homesteader thrice, inflicting severe wounds. Frenchy crawled into his cabin and returned fire, eventually driving the would-be assassin away.

On December 26, 1894, three men rode up to Dog Canyon and onto Frenchy's property. When they approached his cabin, he stepped outside, carrying a rifle. It will never be known what conversation transpired between Frenchy and his visitors, but the result was that he was struck by at least one bullet which mortally wounded him. Frenchy crawled back into his house, climbed up onto his bed, and died.

Two days later, a cowhand named Dan Fletcher reported to the sheriff in La Luz that somebody had killed Frenchy. Justice of the Peace Faustino Acuña organized a coroner's jury, rode out to Dog Canyon, and examined the body. The final determination was that Frenchy had died as a result of a gunshot wound to the chest. Publicly, there was never a word said about who might have done such a horrible thing. Privately, however, suspicion settled on Oliver Lee.

People have short memories it is said, and not too much time passed before few, if any, brought up the subject of Frenchy. In time, the trees in his orchard suffered from lack of water and died. The trail up the foothills to his cabin deteriorated from lack of use.

A Pinkerton detective assigned to the region in 1896 became curious about the killing of Frenchy, and when he had time he investigated aspects of it. It had been related that he sent a report to the governor, even naming the killer, but no response emanated from that office.

According to author A. M. Gibson, Oliver Lee soon obtained a title to Frenchy's claim in Dog Canyon. (A second version of this account provided by author Sonnichsen related that Lee did not acquire a title to the land until ten years later.) Lee constructed more ditches to distribute the water to various locations on his property. Not far from the mouth of Dog Canyon he constructed what was regarded by many as one of the finest homes in the area at the time. In addition, he added barns and corrals and planted an orchard. The site became Lee's ranch headquarters.

13
TENSION BUILDS

The growing tensions between Albert Jennings Fountain and Albert B. Fall, along with those of their respective followers, continued to mount. Customers in certain saloons in Las Cruces were almost entirely Republicans, and in others entirely Democrats. The party members patronized certain stores, barbershops, and liveries and never mixed at any of them It was said that Republicans walked on one side of the streets in Las Cruces and Democrats on the other. Fountain and Fall rarely encountered one another, and when they did it was only in passing and from a distance. This was soon to change, for the two were once again destined to meet in the courtroom.

The former constable Ben Williams was walking through town on his way home when he accidentally encountered Albert Fall who was having a conversation with his brother-in-law, Joe Morgan. An argument immediately raged between the two men, and in the midst of it Morgan pulled a revolver and shot Williams, the bullet slicing some skin from his head behind one ear. So close was Morgan to Williams that the latter suffered powder burns. One report stated that a second later Fall pulled his own handgun and shot Williams in the left elbow. Another report said that Fall did no shooting, that he turned and ducked into a nearby store. Williams, reeling in pain from his wounds, managed to pull his own weapon and fired at Morgan, striking him in the left arm. The entire incident took less than ten seconds, and within moments a crowd had gathered. Fall and Morgan were arrested and immediately released on their own recognizance.

Reasons for the encounter were discussed and debated throughout the town. According to some, all Republicans, Williams was attempting to have Morgan arrested and extradited to Texas where he was apparently wanted for murder. The Fall supporters insisted that Williams just walked up and started shooting. Rumors circulated that Williams had been hired by Fountain to gun down Fall. Fall responded to none of the talk; he merely stated that he did not care for Williams. (Years later Fall and Williams became friends and even conducted business together).

The shooting episode found its way to the Doña Ana County Grand Jury that heard a number of witnesses to the event. The jury decided to indict Williams, along with Albert Jennings Fountain (who was not present at the confrontation), with "intent to murder." District Judge Bantz, suspicious of the leanings of the Democrat-dominated Grand Jury, disapproved of the action.

With enemies such as Oliver Lee and Albert Fall, Ben Williams decided to leave Las Cruces. He moved to El Paso, but he continued working on the cattle rustling cases in the hope of bringing Lee into a courtroom.

Meanwhile, Albert Fountain, in consultation with James Cree, wealthy rancher and the President of the Stock Growers Association, had redoubled his efforts to arrest and bring to trial the cattle rustlers plaguing the Tularosa Basin. In particular, Fountain had his sights set on Oliver Lee. Two months later, Texas law enforcement authorities decided to bring indictments against Lee for cattle rustling. Texas Ranger Captain John R. Hughes was sent to Las Cruces to negotiate with Lee. On arriving in town, Hughes sent for Lee, and Lee arrived for the meeting.

John Hughes was a dogged enforcer of the law and struck fear into the hearts of numerous Texas train robbers and livestock rustlers. He was efficient, effective, and rarely failed to get his man. His reputation spread far and wide, including into New Mexico. Lee, however, was not impressed, and pointed out to Hughes that he had no jurisdiction in New Mexico. Hughes invited Lee to accompany him to Texas to settle matters. Lee refused to go. In a 1943 interview, Hughes told author Sonnichsen that he remembered the encounter well. He stated that Oliver Lee was "pretty full of swagger [and] had everything his own way."

Oliver Lee was indeed a man who was determined to have things his own way. While he would not allow Ranger Hughes to bring him in, he was not opposed to surrendering on his own, which he did on January 8, 1896. He was taken into custody, charged with six criminal acts relating to rustling and brand altering, and released on bond that he posted himself.

During an interview, Lee told a newspaper reporter that he "expected to clear himself without difficulty."

Lee did not turn himself in at El Paso without a plan. Before leaving Las Cruces, he met with his lawyer Albert Fall and discussed a strategy. No sooner had Lee been released than Fall issued a statement to the papers that the source of all of the trouble involving his client was Ben Williams. According to Fall, Williams carried a grudge against the rancher because Lee, acting as a duly appointed deputy, had earlier taken a handgun from him in Las Cruces and that he, Williams, was seeking revenge. The charges against Lee, contended Fall, were entirely manufactured by Williams. It was Williams, said Fall, who arranged for the Texas Rangers to come to Las Cruces in the hope that they would either arrest or kill Oliver Lee. A cattle inspector named Fowler was assigned to examine the cattle in Lee's herd that Williams insisted were stolen. Fowler found no problem with the cattle and also stated that Lee was "one of the straightest stockmen in the Territory."

The charges filed against Lee for cattle rustling did little to quell the animosity between the Fountain and Fall factions. Many supporters of Fall, and thus Lee, resented the attack on one of their leaders. Arguments raged anew over who was to blame for the goings-on.

Bill McNew, along with a couple more of Lee's cowhands, was in El Paso when they learned that cattle detective Les Dow was in town. Dow tread cautiously these days, for word had reached him that Oliver Lee had it in for him. As a result, Dow went around armed. Word soon reached him that McNew and his companions were in town for the specific purpose of killing him and Ben Williams.

On being followed by McNew, Dow stepped into W. A. Irvin's drugstore and explained his dilemma. He told Irvin and an associate that if McNew came after him, to make plans to help him defend himself. Irvin snatched a revolver from under the counter and went up to the second floor where he had a full view of the store. His associate, who remained downstairs, loaded a double-barreled shotgun and kept it ready behind the prescription counter. He had no sooner set the shotgun down when Oliver Lee walked into the store in the company of the city marshal. Spotting Dow, Lee told him he talked to his men, McNew included, and that everything was going to be all right, that he didn't need to worry about anything.

Despite Lee's comment, everything was not going to be all right. For one thing, Dow, along with Ben Williams and C. L. Fowler, all cattle inspectors for the Texas and New Mexico Sanitary Association, had finally secured indictments against Lee and McNew for "unlawful branding and handling of cattle." Assisting Dow, Williams, and Fowler in the courtroom were Texas Rangers Fulgham, Sitter, and Tucker who brought up additional charges. McNew was now in custody and had traveled to Las Cruces to "give bonds for indictments in Doña Ana County...after which he will proceed to surrender himself to El Paso authorities." Should McNew fail to do so, he was to be taken prisoner by the Texas Rangers.

The loop around Lee and his associates that had been cast by Albert Fountain was drawing tighter, and needless to say Lee was none too happy about it. Lee confided to his confederates that he felt he was being specifically targeted by Fountain and persecuted. Something, he determined, needed to be done about Albert Fountain.

Oliver Milton Lee

14
THREATS

Albert Jennings Fountain was convinced that his life was in danger. It has never been clear how he gleaned such a notion. It may have been a gut feeling, a sense of foreboding related to his pursuit of area cattle rustlers, Oliver Lee in particular. On the other hand, Fountain may have heard some gossip, a chance conversation, which led him to believe that certain men wanted him killed.

Fountain was scheduled to travel to Lincoln, New Mexico, to file formal charges in the cattle rustling investigations. A day before he departed Las Cruces, he told his son Jack to retrieve his rifle, a Winchester, clean it and make certain it was in good working order. This done, Fountain took it out behind his house and fired off a few practice rounds. When Jack asked him about his sudden interest in the rifle, Fountain explained that he was certain an attempt was to be made on his life. He told Jack that he did not wish to live in a place where he was forced to carry a weapon all the time, that he had had enough of that in El Paso. He mentioned to his son that the only thing that kept him focused on prosecuting the cattle rustlers was the knowledge that his three sons would avenge his death, should that occur.

Fountain's concern for his life was contagious; his wife and all of his children were likewise worried. The Fountain home was tense with unease and apprehension. At one point, his daughter Maggie, a precocious child with a fondness for playing the piano, noticed a change in her father's demeanor and asked him what was wrong.

Fountain confessed to her that he was in "great danger." Maggie suggested that he not travel to Lincoln alone, that he should take his youngest son, Henry. Henry was eight-years-old and was clearly his father's favorite. Fountain squashed the idea, stating that Henry would just be in the way and that he did not wish to expose him to any danger. Maggie explained that no one would want to cause any trouble if a little boy was along on the trip. Fountain thought it was a bad idea, but the rest of the family chimed in and agreed with Maggie that the child would certainly lessen any threat. Fountain relented and agreed to take the boy.

The following morning, Maggie delivered a note to Henry's teacher excusing him from classes for the next few days. At the same time, a pair of horses was being hitched up to Fountain's buggy. Into the buggy was placed Fountain's dispatch case containing the indictment papers against Oliver Lee and several other men suspected of rustling, a lap robe, a bag of feed for the horses, two rifles, and other gear necessary for the one hundred mile journey across the largely unpopulated landscape to Lincoln. As he was loading equipment into the vehicle, Fountain told his wife that he believed he had a touch of neuralgia and needed something to wrap around his head. She went into the house and returned with a *rebozo,* one that had been in her family for decades. A *rebozo* is a long, flat cloth garment that can be wrapped around the head or upper body to provide warmth. She told him the item was very important to her and to be certain to bring it back.

When Fountain had determined he had everything he needed for the journey, he placed Henry in the buggy seat, climbed in beside him, waved goodbye to his family, slapped the horses with the lines, and rode away down the street. It was the last his family members saw of him, save for oldest son Albert who had occasion to catch up to his father and brother two days later.

After Fountain drove away, daughter Maggie rode out to a ranch near the western slope of the Organ Mountains owned by a Fountain friend, Captain Eugene Van Patten. Maggie was accompanied by an old Mexican woman employed by the Fountain family to serve as chaperone. Patten, along with a partner named Howard Guion, were constructing a hotel on the land, one they hoped would attract travelers to and from Las Cruces. Maggie had two reasons for riding out to the ranch. She liked to work with Patten's horses, and she was enamored of young Guion. The two were discussing becoming engaged.

Maggie Fountain's visit to the ranch proved to be troubling. During her first night she had a dream where she saw her father alone out in the pale dunes of White Sands. Also appearing in her dream was her little brother Henry, whom she adored. When she reached out to hug him, he disappeared.

Maggie, who eventually married Guion, was interviewed by author Sonnichsen on April 10, 1941. She told Sonnichsen that on the night of February 1, 1896, she again dreamed of Henry. She tried once more to embrace him but before she could, Henry said, "Don't touch me. I'm dead." In the dream he went on to say that he had slept between three Texans and just before dawn, one of them said, "Let's get rid of the kid." Henry stated clearly that the one who spoke "has this picture in his pocket. Take a good look at it because he is the one who killed me." In the dream, Henry showed Maggie a picture of a little girl with long, straight black hair and wearing a white dress.

Maggie asked Henry, "What about father?"

Henry replied, "They killed him, too."

15
FOUNTAIN'S FINAL JOURNEY

Fountain's trip to the Lincoln County courthouse got off to an inauspicious start. On the evening of the first day, he and Henry had arrived at a location just beyond San Augustin Pass, about twenty miles northeast of Las Cruces when they were forced to make camp for the night. The two were awakened during the early morning hours when they heard the horses running away. It was not clear to Fountain why they would do such a thing unless they had been frightened off by something, or someone. Fountain was certain the horses would make their way back to Las Cruces and that one of his sons or a neighbor would come to see about him.

Two days later, Fountain's oldest son, Albert, arrived with the horses in tow. Albert told his father how terrified the family was on seeing the horses show up. Before hobbling the animals and preparing to turn in for the night, Fountain asked Albert to take Henry back home with him. Both Albert and Henry argued against the idea so the youth remained with his father.

The following morning after packing the buggy, father and son set out once again for Lincoln. The route took them past Chalk Hill at a point of the White Sands, to Pellman's Well, La Luz, Tularosa, Blazer's Mill near Ruidoso, and finally on to Lincoln and the courthouse.

At the Lincoln County courthouse, cattle detective Les Dow unrolled the calfskin he had acquired from Oliver Lee's herd earlier and spread it out on the floor. He pointed to the evidence that showed how the brand had been altered. This was only one of several demonstrations, and by the time the grand jury was dismissed a few days later, thirty-two indictments had been handed down against men the Southeastern New Mexico Livestock Association identified as rustlers. At the top the list was

Oliver Lee and Bill McNew. Now, thought Fountain, the men who posed a threat to honest cattlemen in the Tularosa Basin would be arrested, tried, and sentenced. Hopefully this would put an end to the problem. Fountain, his work completed, was looking forward to returning home to Las Cruces, to reuniting with his family.

As Fountain was leaving the courtroom, someone he didn't know stepped up and handed him a folded piece of paper. Pausing to read it, Fountain was stunned at the message:

> IF YOU DROP THIS WE WILL BE YOUR FRIENDS.
> IF YOU GO ON WITH IT
> YOU WILL NEVER REACH HOME ALIVE.

After reflecting on the note for a moment, Fountain gathered up Henry and the two climbed into the buggy for the return trip. It was mid-afternoon, January 30, 1896, when Fountain steered the buggy out of the town of Lincoln toward the southwest. He managed eighteen miles before stopping at the home of Dr. J. H. Blazer located near the town of Mescalero. Blazer had been a postmaster and operated a sawmill for years. Like Fountain, he was a former Union Army officer, and the two men enjoyed each other's company. As the evening drew to a close, the subject of the cattle rustling indictments came up. Fountain told Blazer that he had enough evidence to convict the perpetrators, "if they don't make away with me or my witnesses."

As they carried on a conversation about the topic, Blazer expressed concern about Fountain traveling back to Las Cruces in the company of only his son. Blazer offered to send along two friends as guards. Fountain refused the offer, telling Blazer, "I think I can take care of any emergency that may arise." The following morning the two men said their farewells and Fountain hied the horses down the road toward Tularosa.

Fountain had not traveled far out of Mescalero when he drove up to an elderly Apache who was waiting for him along the road. The Indian was holding onto a rope that was attached to a pony. The Indian owed Fountain for previous services, and the pony was an installment on that debt. At first Fountain declined the offer of the pony, saying he had no use for it. The Indian suggested he take it home with him and give it to his children. Fountain was in a hurry and did not wish to discuss the matter, so he accepted the pony and instructed the Apache to tie it to the back of the buggy.

Another mile down the road, Fountain noticed two men trailing him about one hundred yards back. Later when Fountain arrived in Tularosa he parked the buggy next to Dieter's Store and went inside. The two men following him passed by the store and rode out of town.

Fountain and Dieter chatted for a few minutes and the storekeeper invited his guest for lunch. Fountain demurred, stating that he needed to make a few more miles before nightfall. All he needed was some feed for his horses. Dieter sold him forty pounds of oats. From Tularosa, Fountain drove another nine miles to La Luz where he was to spend the night with Dave Sutherland, a town merchant and old friend.

The next morning, February 1, Fountain hitched the horses to the buggy, repacked his belongings and added a lunch prepared by Sutherland's wife. Leaving La Luz, Fountain guided the horses along the road toward the White Sands. It was a cold morning with a strong wind. Fountain and Henry wrapped up in the quilt, the lap robe, and an Indian blanket but still shivered against the elements.

Back on the road, Fountain noticed at once that he appeared to be the object of interest to others. A short distance ahead of him he spotted three riders; two of them rode along one side of the road, the third on the other. They remained just far enough of ahead of him such that he could not identify them or discern any specific characteristics other than that one wore a black hat and the other two wore lighter ones.

Fountain grew concerned. He retrieved his Winchester from behind the seat and laid it across his lap, prepared to use it if necessary. He felt certain he could take care of himself, but he was concerned about Henry should an attack occur. A short time later, he spotted a rider coming toward him. It was a man he knew—Humphrey Hill. The two men pulled up and visited for a few minutes. Fountain confessed to Hill that he was concerned about the men on the road ahead. He told Hill that he had been in Lincoln getting indictments against some cattle rustlers men and that he was in fear that those same men might wish him harm.

Around noon, Fountain pulled the buggy into Pellman's Well not far from White Sands. Fountain remained just long enough to feed and water the horses and take time for a short lunch with Henry.

Two hours later, Fountain encountered Santos Alvarado. Alvarado was a mail carrier who worked out of Tularosa. He had delivered the post to Luna's Well and was returning from that run. When he and Fountain brought up the subject of the horsemen on the road ahead, Alvarado said that when they saw him coming they turned off and galloped away into the desert toward the east in the direction of the Sacramento Mountains. Fountain continued on, passing Luna's Well without stopping and steering the horses down the road toward the southern foothills of the San Andres Mountains where the road stretched on to San Augustín Pass. He was coming up on a location known as Chalk Hill. It will be recalled that in 1894, some of Fountain's targeted suspects had suggested Chalk Hill as a potential ambush site, as revealed by Slick Miller.

As he was approaching Chalk Hill, Fountain encountered Saturnino Barela, another mail carrier. Barela was returning to Las Cruces from a run to Tularosa. Fountain and Barela were friends and enjoyed visiting with one another. Accompanying Barela on this trip were an old man and two women riding in a wagon and a young rider named Fajardo. They had all been taking a break at Chalk Hill and decided to follow Barela into Las Cruces. Just before the party of travelers overtook Fountain, Fajardo called Barela's attention to three horsemen they might encounter on the road ahead. The men were acting in a furtive manner, as though they did not wish to be recognized.

When Barela and his company caught up with Fountain, the colonel pulled to a stop to converse with the mailman, who asked about his family. Barela noted the Winchester laying across Fountain's lap and later recalled that his friend appeared apprehensive. Presently, Fountain asked Barela if he knew those men on the road ahead of them. Barela replied that he did not recognize them, and added that when the horsemen had spotted the mailman and his company they turned off the road as if they did not wish to be seen. Fountain told Barela that the three men had been maintaining their position ahead of the buggy for several miles. He said he feared they were intent on attacking him.

Barela suggested Fountain turn around and travel with him back to Luna's Well where they could spend the night and then resume the trip to Las Cruces together the next morning. Fountain considered the mailman's suggestion for several moments, then stated that he felt that he needed to get to Las Cruces that evening. He told Barela he would continue on and "take my chances." Fountain said goodbye to Barela, snapped the lines, and headed toward Chalk Hill. It was late afternoon.

16
AMBUSH

The sun was descending toward the western horizon as Fountain approached Chalk Hill. With around two hours of daylight remaining, he hoped to make San Augustin Pass before dark. From there, the remainder of the trip would be relatively short and downhill.

The desert landscape here is open and flat for miles around, the views wide and expansive. Yucca, creosote, and clumps of brush dot the relatively featureless environment. Here and there, slight variations in the landscape occur, one of which was Chalk Hill. Chalk Hill is not so much a hill as it is a slight rise in the otherwise featureless plain. Not far away toward the north was White Sands, an extensive array of weathered gypsum sands the persistent desert winds had formed into spectacular, shining dunes, a remnant of an ancient sea bottom.

As Fountain steered the buckboard toward Chalk Hill, it is likely that he still carried the Winchester across his lap. Henry was perched to his right on the wooden spring seat. The dispatch case carrying the indictments for Oliver Lee and other cattle rustlers was riding under the seat. Approaching Chalk Hill from the northeast, one has a fine view of the surrounding area save for one location—the area immediately on the opposite, downhill side of the rise. A man standing on the road at that location would not be seen until the traveler was at the top of the rise.

As the buckboard crested Chalk Hill, Fountain saw nothing or no one, least of all the man who was hidden in a clump of brush several yards south of the hill and off to his left. The man was Todd Bailey, the nephew of Oliver Lee. Bailey had proven himself an excellent marksman and had been enlisted by his uncle to take out his nemesis, Albert Fountain. Bailey was seventeen years old.

Not far away but out of sight, three horsemen sat their saddles and waited for what was to come. Researchers have debated the identity of the horsemen, but most have narrowed it down to a choice between James Gilliland, Bill, McNew, Ed Brown, and Oliver Lee. It has been suggested and argued that Lee was not among the three, but was stationed a short distance away. (Ed Brown, in a statement to George Curry, claimed Oliver Lee was involved in the plot to kill Fountain, but was not at Chalk Hill at the time of the murder.)

According to Bailey family members, as the buckboard began the descent down the gentle slope of Chalk Hill, Todd Bailey raised his rifle and sighted on Fountain. Just as the buckboard reached the bottom of the slope, he fired two shots. At least one bullet from Bailey's rifle struck Fountain, a mortal wound.

An alternative version of this event exists, one credited to Jim Gilliland and related to author Leon Metz in a 1969 interview with Butler Oral Burris, a friend of Gilliland's. According to Burris, Gilliland stated that he, Oliver Lee, and Bill McNew took up pursuit of Fountain as he was arriving near the uphill (northeast) portion of Chalk Hill. All three men, using rifles, shot at Fountain, at least one bullet striking him in the back. According to Burris, Gilliland stated that Fountain "looked just like an old bullfrog when he jumped between the horses [pulling the buckboard]."

Some have questioned this second version of the attack on Fountain. For one thing, this tactic makes little sense for the speeding wagon would have made Fountain a difficult target. It has also been argued that the intent may have been to chase Fountain to a point near Bailey, and should Bailey miss his target, the three horsemen were thus in a position to overtake the buckboard and kill Fountain. Another reason for the skepticism applied to this version is that, according to acquaintances, Gilliland was reputed to misrepresent accounts of his past on occasion.

Whatever the cause of Fountain's wounding, the reaction he made caused the team of horses to veer sharply to the left (east) where the road leveled out from the hill's slope. At this point, Fountain was either dead or dying. The horses raced another few dozen yards before stopping. According to the tracks found at the scene, three men rode up to the buckboard moments later and surrounded it. It has been suggested on the basis of tracks that they were joined by a fourth man on foot. The fourth man was likely Todd Bailey. At this point, a decision needed to be made: Eight-year-old Henry Fountain was still alive and was a witness to the killing. Seated in the buggy, he looked into the faces of the men surrounding him, men who were responsible for killing his father. In turn, the men regarded the boy, and nervously came to the realization that he would have to be dealt with.

Albert Jennings Fountain had just completed his final journey in life. His corpse, however, was on the verge of undertaking another, a long and bizarre journey, and one that had numerous stops along the way.

It was imperative that the killers get the buckboard containing the presumed dead Fountain and his son far from the main road. This well-used route saw travelers, freighters, mail carriers, and others, and a rider could arrive at any minute. Taking the lead lines to Fountain's team of horses, the riders continued eastward. After traveling for much of the night, they finally reined in and settle in for the night at a location called Horse Camp Mesa. By the time the killers had arrived at the site, they were joined by Oliver Lee. Here, Fountain's body was pulled from the buckboard and placed on a blanket that had been spread out on the ground nearby. The pony that had been tied to the rear of the vehicle was turned loose, and it trotted away to the north. A fire was started and a coffeepot set onto the coals.

One can only imagine the terror that filled young Henry Fountain. Based on footprints later found at the scene, it was apparent that the boy was still alive at this point. Around the campsite that evening as the men drank coffee and smoked cigarettes, they discussed what must be done with Henry. They only conclusion they felt they could arrive at was to eliminate all witnesses, which meant that the boy had to be killed, a task that appealed to none of them. They decided to draw straws to determine who would execute the lad. Jim Gilliland drew the short straw.

Henry was seated not far away. It will never be known if he overheard the conversation between the men. After finishing his cigarette, Gilliland rose from his position near the fire. With his back to Henry, he withdrew a pocketknife and opened it, the three-inch blade gleaming in the firelight. Holding the knife against one leg, Gilliland casually walked away from the campfire and circled around to a point behind Henry. Without hesitating, Gilliland grabbed the boy by the hair with his left hand, pulled his head back, and slit his throat.

According to a forensic detective, it is likely that Henry screamed. His normal reaction would have been for his hands to come up, his right hand grabbing Gilliland's shirtsleeve as his throat was laid open. Blood gushed from the wound onto Gilliland's knife hand. The oxygenated blood was bright red. When Henry's windpipe was severed, the scream was cut off, turning to a gurgling moan. The boy's body went rigid for a second or two, the grip on Gilliland's sleeve tightened, then went limp. Gilliland released his hold on Henry's hair and the boy dropped to the sandy ground, bleeding to death.

Though this sequence is gruesome, it gets worse; Henry did not die instantly. With his external and internal jugular veins cut, Henry would bleed to death. But it would take another fifteen to twenty seconds before the blood would stop feeding his brain and he would lapse into unconsciousness. He would remain alive for another two to three minutes.

After sunrise the following day, the killers awoke, made coffee, and made plans to depart. The bodies of Albert and Henry Fountain were tied to the backs of horses. After the campfire had been doused, the riders saddled up and traveled eastward toward the Jarilla Mountains. The buckboard was left behind at Horse Camp Mesa. Close to the base of Culp Peak, located farther north in the Sacramento Mountains, was a steam-operated water pump. Adjacent to the pump was the boiler. The water pumped from the well went to nearby tank from which cattle drank. It was to this location the riders guided their horses, their grisly cargo in tow.

The two bodies were placed inside the firebox of the boiler and a fire started. The door to the firebox was closed tightly, thus causing the oxygen to be depleted. Thus, the fire died and there was no direct flame to the bodies, just heat. The bodies were rendered; the fat melted away and the muscles and tendons shrank, causing the corpses to shrivel. The bodies remained in the boiler for the night.

The next morning, the fire door was opened. The bodies were pulled out and wrapped in blankets. They were taken to Oliver Lee's Dog Canyon Ranch and buried in the peach orchard that was located only a few dozen yards in front of the house. Nearby was a hog pen in which Lee kept a number of swine. Once or twice each year a few hogs were butchered, the best cuts of the meat hung in the smokehouse, and the rest turned into sausage. Lee had the hogs turned loose to root around in the orchard in order to disguise the grave.

Unexpectedly, the hogs rooted up the corpse of Henry Fountain at the same time that Lucy Gilliland, the sister of Jim Gilliland, stepped out of the house and walked into the orchard. She said something to her brother who, disturbed at the reappearance of the bodies, determined to relocate them. It is not clear if Gilliland informed Oliver Lee of the discovery, but since it occurred in Lee's front yard, it is presumed that he did. Gilliland, along with Bill McNew, disinterred the corpses and transported them to James Canyon near the northern edge of the Sacramento Mountains where they were reburied, and hopefully for the last time. As it turned out, this was not to be the case. (See "Background on Page 187.")

Todd Bailey

17
THE DISAPPEARANCE OF ALBERT JENNINGS FOUNTAIN

After leaving Colonel Fountain on the road to Las Cruces, mail carrier Saturnino Barela continued on to Luna's Well where he spent the night. As he prepared to turn in for the night, his thoughts were occupied with Fountain's concern over the notion that he might be in danger. Barela worried for the colonel and for his son, Henry. The next morning, Barela rose, prepared a small breakfast, and hitched his horses to his wagon as he waited for Santos Alvarado to arrive with the mail from Tularosa bound for Las Cruces. Following the exchange of the mail, Barela set out on the road back the way he had come.

After passing Chalk Hill, Barela spotted the tracks of Fountain's buggy in the road. And then, only a short distance from the end of the downhill slope of Chalk Hill, he noted that the tracks left the road and veered sharply to the east and into the scrub. Barela pulled his wagon to a halt, stepped to the ground, and followed the tracks. Thirty to forty yards later, the mailman saw where the tracks of three horses had approached those of the buggy. Recalling Fountain's earlier concern over the three riders that had been on the road ahead of him, Barela feared that the colonel had encountered some kind of disaster. He rushed back to his wagon and made haste to Las Cruces where he reported what he saw.

The Fountain household was in turmoil. Oldest son Albert was beside himself with worry. He located brother Jack and his father-in-law Antonio Garcia, along with several friends, and quickly saddled horses in preparation for the long ride out to Chalk Hill in spite of the fact that night had fallen. In addition, the temperature had dropped to below zero and a strong cold wind was blowing in from the northwest.

After Albert and company departed, Major W. H. H. Llewellyn of the territorial militia organized another group including Captain Van Patten, Lew Gans, Henry Stoes, Deputy Sheriff John Casey, James Baird, Fred Bascom, and Robert Ellwood. Llewellyn arranged for a buckboard to transport provisions, though both this party, as well as the one organized by Albert Fountain, manifested such haste that few of the participants had time to pack food, water, feed for their horses, and blankets. Both groups arrived at a campsite on the eastern slope of San Augustin Pass where they rested men and horses alike.

The following morning, February 3, Albert Fountain and Antonio Garcia rode to Luna's Well. There, they were told that Fountain had passed through there on Saturday. The two men returned down the road and joined the rest of the party that had set up camp at Parker's Well, not far from the Cox ranch. Following a brief discussion, all rode on to Chalk Hill, determined to pick up the trail of Fountain's buggy.

On arriving at Chalk Hill, members of the party dismounted and walked about the area in search of evidence. Not far from where Fountain's buggy tracks left the road, one of the men found a place where someone had hidden behind a bush and out of sight of any travelers. This was the spot Todd Bailey had chosen for the ambush. From this vantage point, the observer had a clear view of the road as it passed through the cut. Two empty rifle cartridges were found at the site, both recently fired.

Others followed the buggy tracks where they abruptly turned off the road approximately one hundred yards from the base of Chalk Hill. The prints of the pony that had been tied behind the buggy showed where the animal had shied away from the vehicle as though frightened by something, likely the gunshots fired by Bailey. For reasons known only to them, members of the party deduced that whoever had been hidden behind the bush had stopped Fountain while the three horsemen approached the buggy and encircled it. The tracks indicated that the riders and the buggy proceeded away from the road for another one hundred yards before stopping. At this point, discarded cigarette butts indicated that all remained at this location for about an hour.

It was at this location that a subsequent investigative party found blood. Tularosan John P. Meadows was examining the area when he found a patch of old blood several inches wide. Blood had soaked into the unconsolidated desert sands to a depth of nearly a foot, according to Meadows. This represented a great deal of blood, and whoever had lost it did not live long.

Several others claimed to have found the patch of dried blood. According to Van Patten, Nicolas Armijo said he found it when the two men were examining the area on February 10. Patten later denied that it was Armijo who found the blood. Two men—Abran Gamboa and Manuel Parra—had also been given credit for finding the blood.

Meadows advanced a theory of his own with regard to the event. He speculated that Fountain was shot where the buggy had stopped. He further theorized that Fountain's blood had collected in his buttoned up overcoat and that later he had been thrown from the buggy onto the ground where the blood seeped out. According to Meadows, there were indications that a blanket had been placed next to the bloodstain and something heavy laid upon it.

From the location of the bloodstain, the tracks of the buggy continued eastward into the sand dunes. The search party followed the tracks for miles. Late that afternoon, they came upon the buckboard. It had been abandoned twelve miles east of Chalk Hill. At this location it was clear that whoever attacked Fountain had gone through all of his possessions. According to the Pinkerton Report, Fountain's rifle was missing. (At least one account states that Fountain was carrying two rifles.) Also missing were his dagger and canteen, as well as his lap robe and Indian blanket. Even a utility rope and some spare leather straps were missing. Fountain's wooden dispatch case was there, but it had been opened and every paper in it was missing. Among the papers were the indictments, as well as all of the pertinent evidence, for a number of cattle rustlers, in particular Oliver Lee and Bill McNew.

The suitcase Fountain carried was still there but much of what it originally contained was gone. Henry's hat was in it. Under the buggy seat, searchers found the *rebozo* Fountain's wife had given him for warmth. Also found lying inside the buggy was the threatening note that had been passed to Fountain at the Lincoln County courthouse.

The search party continued to follow the trail which led eastward. Five miles later and seventeen miles from Chalk Hill, they came upon a campsite. From the sign encountered, it was apparent that three men had remained there, made a fire, and cooked a meal. Once again, there was an indication that a blanket had been laid out on the ground and a heavy object placed upon it.

According to the tracks found at the campsite, one of the men wore a boot with a badly worn heel. Major Llewellyn cut sticks to match the lengths of the boot tracks but later lost them. Among the tracks of the three men were those of a young boy who was apparently wearing only one shoe. Having determined all that could be learned at the campsite, the posse pushed on.

The search party continued eastward, gradually approaching the Jarilla Mountains, a north-south oriented low and narrow range of granite and limestone and containing numerous rugged, rocky passes. Ten miles beyond the Jarillas lay the Sacramento Mountains. Between the Jarillas and the Sacramentos lay Oliver Lee's ranches. One, named Wildy Well, was just on the east side of the Jarillas. The other ranch, the larger one and the headquarters, was called the Dog Canyon Ranch and was located just west of the Sacramento Mountains and near the mouth of Dog Canyon.

As the posse followed the tracks of the suspects, it was noted that they suddenly diverged as they approached the Jarilla Mountains. One set of tracks, a lone rider, peeled off from the rest and went southeastward through a pass that led to Wildy Well. The other set of tracks—two horsemen who were leading one of Fountain's horses—headed for the upper, or northernmost pass, a trail that would take them to Oliver Lee's Dog Canyon Ranch. By this time, snow had begun to fall and the sun was setting. After traveling through the northernmost pass, the posse stopped to set up camp and prepared to spend a cold night before resuming their tracking. The searchers were low on provisions and water.

At sunrise, several of the searchers decided to return to their homes. Taking the buckboard, they headed back to Las Cruces. Five men decided to continue the search. They were Major Llewellyn, Thomas Brannigan, John Casey, Lew Gans, and Henry Stoes. Just after they broke camp and set out, Brannigan shot an antelope, so they stopped long enough to butcher the animal and cook breakfast. Following the meal, they set out once again, following the trail toward Oliver Lee's headquarters ranch.

As Llewellyn and his men turned north toward the Dog Canyon Ranch, Carl Clausen, Fountain's son-in-law, and Luis Herrera came through the pass in the Jarilla Mountains. The two men were also on a mission to try to find clues relative to the colonel's disappearance. Instead of following the posse northward, the pair turned south toward Wildy Well. On their way, they came upon the tracks of the solitary horseman who had turned in that direction earlier.

When Clausen and Herrera arrived at Wildy Well, they encountered five men who were hanging around the house. The five did not detect the two oncoming riders until they were almost upon them, and when they did, the five scrambled into the house. As Clausen and Herrera sat their horses and looked around, the men slowly exited the structure. Among them was Oliver Lee. Clausen asked Lee if they could water their horses at the well. Lee granted them permission to do so, and then asked, "What are you fellows after?"

Clausen told him about the mysterious disappearance of Colonel Fountain and his son and that they were looking for him. Clausen asked Lee if he would join them in their search. Lee responded that he did not have the time, and then cursed Fountain. Lee acted neither surprised that Fountain was missing, nor was he in the least bit concerned. Lee then turned, mounted his horse, and rode toward the Jarilla Mountains.

Meanwhile, a few miles to the north the other search party stopped for a discussion. Stoes told Llewellyn that he was a friend of Oliver Lee and that they should ride to his ranch headquarters and ask him if he knew anything about the disappearance of Colonel Fountain. As they talked, one of Lee's cattle herds approached. Driven by ranch hands Dan Fitchett and W. T. White, the herd massed over the trail the search party had been following, obliterating any and all tracks. Llewellyn thought this was a calculated move, a decision made by Oliver Lee.

For reasons unclear, Llewellyn refused to travel to the Dog Canyon Ranch. Instead, he argued that Wildy Well was closer and that the horses were in dire need of water. The truth is, water could be found at both locations, and the distance to each was about the same. From Wildy Well, explained Llewellyn, they would return to Las Cruces. They arrived at the well around four o'clock in the afternoon and set up camp. It was so cold, however, that three searchers elected to pack up and continue on to Las Cruces. They were forced to stop every few miles to build a fire and get warm. Around four o'clock in the morning, they made it to the W. W. Cox Ranch where they were invited inside and out of the weather.

When Llewellyn and his group arrived back in Las Cruces, they related their tales of the search. Llewellyn posited that the bodies of Fountain and his son had been carried on the backs of Fountain horses toward the Sacramento Mountains. Up until that point many people had held out some hope that Fountain and his son would be found alive.

18
SUSPICION

With the news that something dreadful likely happened to Colonel Fountain and his son Henry, suspicion immediately focused on Fountain's two most obvious rivals—Oliver Lee and Albert Fall. When someone is murdered, one of the first questions asked by law enforcement is: Who stands to benefit from the death? In the case of Fountain, an obvious beneficiary of his removal would have been Oliver Lee. Lee was well aware of the fact that Fountain had specifically targeted him in his quest to arrest and bring to trial cattle rustlers throughout the Tularosa Basin, and possessed enough evidence to have him arrested, indicted, and likely sent to prison. Along with Fountain's disappearance, the paperwork pertaining to the evidence against Lee was missing. With Fountain gone, Les Dow was now the only person who was in possession of said evidence. This made the cattle detective a marked man.

Albert Fall regarded Fountain as an enemy, one who would thwart his own political desires and ambitions. Given their past relationship, and given the hate each had for the other, Fall would have been relieved, if not gratified, at Fountain's removal. The fact that Albert Fall was Oliver Lee's attorney did not go unnoticed.

Fall, in fact, owned a gold mine seven miles from Chalk Hill, and that fact alone was to render him complicit in Fountain's disappearance in the minds of some. Fall was allegedly at or near the mine at the time of Fountain's disappearance. In truth, Fall often visited the mine in a supervisory capacity.

More suspicion fell on Oliver Lee via the person of Mrs. Eva Taylor. One week following Fountain's disappearance, Mrs. Taylor had an affidavit made in Lincoln relative to what she claimed to know. Taylor stated that on the night of Fountain's disappearance she was riding on a stage toward

La Luz with another mail carrier, Alvino Guerra. Around four in the morning as the stage approached La Luz, Taylor said she spotted three horsemen crossing the road ahead of the stage. She identified two of them as Oliver Lee and Bill McNew. She said she thought the third man was Frank Chatfield but could not be certain.

A ranch hand named Jack Maxwell was employed at the Lee ranch. Maxwell stated that he was at the ranch on Saturday and Sunday, February 1 and 2, and that he observed Lee, McNew, and James Gilliland ride in "on fagged horses after dark Saturday." To Maxwell, the trio appeared "very nervous and ill at ease." According to Maxwell, Lee and Gilliland slept out in the brush and that he bunked inside with McNew.

It was also learned that after Lee and posse member Clausen exchanged a few words at the Wildy Well Ranch house, Lee mounted his horse and rode away, arriving later at Albert Fall's gold mine camp. Fountain sympathizers thought this suspicious.

The February 14, 1896 issue of the *Rio Grande Republican,* an unabashedly pro-Fountain newspaper, lost no time in calling for the arrest and execution of Oliver Lee, who at that time was in Las Cruces. While there, Lee encountered Phil Fall, brother to Albert. Phil informed Lee that he was a wanted man, that there were warrants out for him, McNew, Gilliland, and Jack Tucker. Lee and Phil Fall went to the office of Justice of the Peace Valdez and asked for the warrants. Valdez told the two men to return the next day. Instead, they went to see District Attorney R. F. Young. Young was unaware of the existence of the warrants. A short time later, Lee encountered Sheriff Guadalupe Ascarate who suggested that he should get out of town as soon as possible, to return to his ranch. Lee heeded Ascarate's advice and rode back his Wildy Well ranch. The following day, District Attorney Young sent a messenger to the ranch informing Lee that the indictments had been dismissed.

Meanwhile, searchers combing the desert in the area of the disappearance reported finding Fountain's two horses. The left side of one of them was stained red, presumably by blood. It was assumed that this was likely the horse that was transporting the body of Fountain.

Tensions, already high and tight, were mounting. There were threats directed toward both Lee and Albert Fall, but never to their faces. Lee and Fall were heard stating that they believed men had been hired to kill them. Author Sonnichsen wrote:

> Both sides were so worked up that small scraps of fact or rumor ballooned into fantastic and blood-curdling histories of plot and counterplot. Any man who knew something, or thought he knew something, was quoted extensively. Each new detail fanned the embers of all the old suspicions and grudges and enmities. Friends were friends no longer. Neighbors ceased to be neighborly. And men who had never carried guns before began to pack them now.

The investigation into the disappearance of Colonel Albert Jennings Fountain had stalled. A large percentage of those combing the desert country for evidence were interested and eager, but untrained and inexperienced. The elected and appointed law enforcement authorities were largely inept or simply unwilling to assume responsibility for the investigation. Governor William T. Thornton was following the process and progress of the investigation, or lack of it, and was growing interested and concerned. A breakthrough was needed. It was time to enlist the assistance of a trained and experienced lawman.

James Gililland

19
RE-ENTER LES DOW

During the weeks following the disappearance of Albert Jennings Fountain passions cooled down somewhat but did not disappear. Suspicions fomented and accusations were hurled during discussions and arguments, but little had been accomplished toward officially identifying the abductors and presumed murderers of Albert Jennings Fountain and his son, Henry. As progress on this front stalled, there evolved an interesting juxtapositioning of events in El Paso, Texas.

It was not unusual for residents of Las Cruces and other nearby New Mexico towns to visit El Paso from time to time. The city offered distractions and delights not to be found in the outlying areas, entertainments ranging from gambling to opera. Across the border in Juarez, Mexico, bullfighting tempted some, as did the variety of entertainment venues and drinking and dining establishments, as well as houses of prostitution.

During the spring of 1896, El Paso was being touted as the location for a heavyweight boxing match that was to decide the world champion. Bob Fitzsimmons, who was the reigning titleholder, would defend his belt against Peter Maher, the Irish national champion. The fight was attracting gamblers and hucksters to El Paso, and the town's law enforcement authorities were fielding complaints from the citizenry. The promoter of the bout, Dan Stuart, did little to assuage the concerns of the law enforcement officials. Stuart had previously been run out of Arizona, New Mexico, and even Mexico. As the days wore on, the likelihood of the bout taking place in El Paso was growing dimmer.

As El Paso was only a one-hour train ride away from Las Cruces, residents of that town flocked to the big city to participate in the goings on as well as to conduct business. Ben Williams, late of the brief gunfight with Albert Fall, was now a resident of El Paso. Oliver Lee visited El Paso often to conduct business and have meetings with a variety of men.

Lee had another reason to visit El Paso so often. According to a report filed with the Pinkerton National Detective Agency on March 15, 1896, by operative J. C. Fraser, Oliver Lee "lays up" with a woman during his trips. On March 18, Fraser reported that the woman's name was "Mrs. Stevens, a widow," who operated a rooming house on San Antonio Street.

The three Fountain sons—Albert, Jack, and Tom—were also no strangers to El Paso. The sons were eager to see justice done relative to their father and little brother, and were frustrated at the delays in the investigation. The boys were inclined to enact justice themselves, and though their enmity was focused on Oliver Lee and Albert Fall, they had no proof of the involvement of the men.

At one point, Fall arranged a meeting with the oldest Fountain son, Albert, Jr. According to one source, Fall convinced young Albert that he, Fall, had nothing to do with the disappearance of his father and brother. Jack Fountain, however, was not as easily swayed. Despite Albert Fountain's revised position in the matter, Jack still viewed Fall as complicit in the disappearance and presumed killing. Jack Fountain had taken to hanging around Ben Williams, who naturally had little use for Fall. On one occasion, Jack and Ben, carrying rifles, traveled to El Paso allegedly in search of Albert Fall. Fall was warned to be wary of the two.

Two days after Jack Fountain and Ben Williams arrived in El Paso, Oliver Lee and Tom Tucker showed up. For a few tense hours many in town were convinced that Lee and Jack Fountain were on the verge of confronting one another, but nothing happened. Coincidentally, cattle inspector Les Dow also happened to be in El Paso. The city was fairly bustling with individuals involved one way or another in the Fountain case.

On February 19, boxing promoter Stuart, realizing he would be unable to hold the championship fight in El Paso, accepted an invitation from Judge Roy Bean of Langtry, Texas, to stage the contest there on a narrow sandy island in the middle of the Rio Grande. The tiny town of Langtry sat between the railroad tracks and the river. On February 20, the train carried carloads of eager boxing fans from El Paso to the dusty West Texas town. It was earlier determined that there would be a need for a cadre of lawmen to maintain crowd order. To that end, the United States marshal in El Paso appointed Oliver Lee, Bill McNew, and Jim Gilliland as deputies.

When Les Dow learned of the appointments, he grew enraged. He stormed down to the railroad station platform and addressed the crowd of boxing fans awaiting the train, among them the U. S. marshal. Dow confronted the marshal and, according to a newspaper report, said, "What on earth do you mean by making deputies out of these men? Don't you know who they are?" The allusion, of course, was to their alleged role in the disappearance and presumed murder of Colonel Fountain. Dow continued his rant by calling out Lee, Gilliland, and McNew and inviting either of them, "or any two," to step up and have it out with him. None of the three new deputies were in the crowd.

Nearly two weeks later, Dow spotted Lee in an El Paso bar and walked up to him. According to Jack Fountain, Dow told Lee that this thing between them had gone far enough and that he was ready to settle it, "peacefully or otherwise, but there has to be an end to it." In response, Lee extended his hand and invited Dow to shake on it.

The significance of Lee's offer to shake is unclear. It was because of Dow's investigation of altered cattle brands that Lee and his compatriots were indicted. Lee was not likely to forget such a thing.

Three months later, Les Dow was murdered.

Les Dow

20
THE KILLING OF LES DOW

James Leslie "Les" Dow was born in Clinton, Texas, near San Antonio in 1860. Dow had a varied career before becoming a cattle inspector. After arriving in New Mexico he worked as a hotel manager and then as a saloon keeper before becoming a deputy sheriff in Chaves County. Later, he was hired as a range detective and cattle inspector for the Texas and New Mexico Sanitary Association. In 1884, Dow was hired as a brand inspector for the Southwestern Livestock Association. In 1885, he purchased a ranch west of Seven Rivers, New Mexico. He also operated a saloon in town. One evening in April 1891, a drunk named Zach Light approached Dow in the bar and demanded money. When Dow refused, Light pulled a handgun and fired a shot at Dow, missing wide. Dow reached for his own weapon and shot Light, killing him. Dow was charged with murder, pled self-defense, and was acquitted.

In 1886, Dow was elected sheriff of Eddy County, New Mexico, while holding a commission as a deputy U. S. marshal. He took office on January 1, 1897. One of his first tasks was to investigate cattle thefts in the area, and his primary suspect was a man named Dave Kemp, who had served as sheriff 1890-1892. In February, Dow arrested Kemp; the charge was "carrying a gun." Dow and Kemp were subsequently described as "bitter enemies" from that point on.

David Leon Kemp was a native of Coleman County, Texas. Years earlier he had been sentenced to twenty-five years in prison for murder. While incarcerated, he helped to thwart a prison break and was given an early release. A short time later, Kemp moved to Eddy County, New Mexico, where he was later elected sheriff.

In February 1887, Les Dow was killed. The incident is controversial and a number of different versions have been offered. Even the date of the killing is disputed.

According to writer Leon Metz, Les Dow and Dave Kemp fought a duel on February 16, 1897. Metz stated that as Dow attempted draw his revolver, the weapon became snagged in the holster. Kemp pulled his own weapon and fired, the bullet striking Dow in the mouth. Les Dow died the following day. Concentrated investigation and research into this version has yielded only hearsay, and no evidence was found suggesting that such a thing ever happened.

The writer Jay Robert Nash provides an alternate version. Nash claims Dow was shot down in Carlsbad in April 1897 "while scanning a pile of letters in the postal station." Nash identified the killer as David Kemp, who subsequently fled from the building. There were no witnesses to the event as described by Nash.

Another writer, Don Bullis, stated that on the evening of February 18, 1897, Dow was walking out of the post office when he was shot in the face at close range. The version offered by Bullis has Kemp and a man named Will Kennon hiding in a doorway not far from the post office where they were waiting for Dow to exit. When the sheriff appeared, states Bullis, Kemp shot him and fled. Constable Dee Harkey arrived at the scene a few minutes after the shooting. He spoke to the dying Dow who told him that he did not see the killer "because the muzzle flash from the gun, so close to his face, temporarily blinded him." Dave Kemp was immediately suspected by Harkey of killing Dow because of the well-known enmity between the two men. Kemp was arrested, tried, and subsequently acquitted. In the end, it was learned that no one saw the shooter or witnessed the killing.

The above versions of the killing of Les Dow provide more questions than answers, and following an analysis of all three it is easy to conclude that no one knows what actually occurred and who was responsible since it was witnessed by no one. To add to the controversy there is yet another version.

Oliver Lee, Jim Gilliland, and Bill McNew had been identified by Les Dow as cattle rustlers as well as principals in an extensive cattle rustling operation. Dow provided evidence against the three, as well as more than a dozen others. The entire case against Lee and his compatriots revolved around Dow and the information he possessed. If Dow was eliminated, then the case against Lee *et al* would be significantly weakened. Kill Dow, reasoned Lee, and the result would be a break in the chain of evidence.

According to the descendants of Todd Bailey, Oliver Lee's nephew and devoted employee, Lee sent Bailey, along with notorious assassin Jim

Miller, to Carlsbad to eliminate Dow. The two men waiting in hiding for Dow to come out of the post office were not Kemp and Kennon, but Bailey and Miller. When Dow appeared, Todd Bailey shot him in the face with a revolver. Dow died the following day.

Within seconds after the shooting, Bailey and Miller mounted their horses and raced away. After riding two miles out of town, Bailey and Miller stopped, pulled the shoes off of their horses, and turned them out to graze among a nearby herd of cattle. In the event that a pursuing posse following the tracks caught up with them, there would be no hoof prints to compare. Two days later when they were certain there was no pursuit, the horses were gathered, reshod, and the two returned to the Lee ranch, their assignment completed.

Jim Miller

21
ENTER PAT GARRETT

During the mid-1890s, Pat Garrett was still, and only, known to most as the killer of the outlaw, Billy the Kid. It was a claim he made himself, one that was disputed at the scene by one of the two deputies that accompanied him, and years later by the second. Garrett's claim is repeated today by western outlaw and lawman enthusiasts, in large part based on material they have read over the years or movies that they have watched. The claim has been stated and re-stated so often that is become part and parcel of the fabric of western American lore and accepted as fact.

In recent years, professional research and investigation have yielded substantial and compelling evidence that points to the reality that Pat Garrett lied. (See *Billy the Kid: Beyond the Grave, Pat Garrett: The Man Behind the Badge,* and *Billy the Kid: Investigating History's Mysteries.)* The evidence was always there; it was simply overlooked and/or misinterpreted by those who claim to be historians.

Following his alleged shooting of Billy the Kid, Garrett's law enforcement career, along with his political ambitions, declined markedly. He was defeated in elections. He was also deeply in debt and owed money to a number of individuals, including some well-placed politicians, debts he never paid off. Furthermore, Garrett was a notorious drunk, an adulterer, and an inveterate gambler who lost more than he won. Garrett had a tendency to lie that bordered on pathological. At the time of the disappearance of Albert Jennings Fountain, Garrett was living on a ranch in Uvalde, Texas.

Garrett was acquainted with the Fountain case as a result of reading newspaper accounts. In addition, he heard rumors that he was being considered as one who could lead a reliable investigation into the matter. Because of Garrett's shoddy reputation as well as his declining credibility, many have wondered why he would be regarded as a candidate for such a responsibility. The reasons are likely two-fold. First, the Doña Ana County sheriff's department, which had jurisdiction over the kidnapping, was known to be less than capable. The current sheriff, Guadalupe Ascarate, was considered a tool of the Democratic politicians, and his deputies amounted to little more than hired gunmen. Ascarate had little experience with, or success at, law enforcement and was regarded by many as incompetent.

Second, it was becoming apparent that New Mexico Governor William T. Thornton was close to inviting Garrett's participation. Thornton was, above all else, a politician. Garrett may not have been the most qualified choice for heading the investigation, but he was still regarded as a bit of a celebrity. Thornton was not convinced that the lawman, on his own, would experience any success relative to the Fountain case. What Garrett had going for him, however, was his lingering reputation among some as a fearless lawman. As a result, he could still generate headlines. Politicians of the time, just like today, desired to be the subject of, or close to those who generated, headlines.

In El Paso, Thornton met with a delegation to discuss the matter of inviting Garrett's participation. In addition to Thornton, the group included Major W. H. H. Llewellyn, District Clerk George Curry, Albert Fall, Sheriff Ascarate, along with others, all regarded as prominent politicians of one stripe or another. Initially, the discussions reached dead ends. Albert Fall let it be known that he considered the process a farce. In the end, however, an agreement was finally arrived at, and Governor Thornton sent a telegram to Garrett at his ranch inviting him to a meting in El Paso. Garrett bought a train ticket and arrived in the city on February 20, about the time it was decided to move the Fitzsimmons-Maher fight to Langtry. The governor and Garrett met and discussed aspects of the case. When Thornton returned to the New Mexico capital, he made a formal recommendation that Garrett be appointed a chief deputy in charge of the Fountain investigation and receive a salary of $500 per month. In desperate need of money, Garrett accepted.

Things began to go bad for Garrett almost immediately on his arrival at Las Cruces. Sheriff Ascarate was opposed to Garrett's involvement from the beginning and openly resented what he regarded as an intrusion into the operations of his office. He also stated that he did not like being told who his deputies would be. Numa Reymond recommended that Ascarate resign and Garrett be appointed sheriff.

Thornton pressured District Judge Banz to remove Ascarate from office, which he managed to do a few days later. Numa Reymond was installed in the office. It was expected that Reymond would make Garrett chief deputy and then resign so that he could then step into the job. Once in office, however, Reymond decided he wanted to keep the position.

On February 24, Garrett was again invited to El Paso for a meeting with a number of prominent New Mexicans, a meeting called by and presided over by Governor Thornton. There, an agreement was made for Garrett to pursue the Fountain case as a private detective. He was told he would be paid $8,000 if he was successful in obtaining an arrest and conviction plus $150 per month for expenses. He was also promised an opportunity to be considered for the office of sheriff when the appropriate time came. Garrett accepted the offer. Garrett's motivation for accepting the position was to fulfill his ego as well as providing him with some much-needed financial resources. He was broke, saddled with massive gambling debts as well as debts from personal loans, and his drinking and whoring habits were costing more money than he had to spend. Garrett moved his family to Las Cruces. Four years later he sold his Uvalde ranch to future vice presidential candidate John Nance Garner.

Garrett was unprepared for the criticism that followed his appointment. Elfego Baca, a colorful lawman from Socorro, loudly proclaimed that Governor Thornton had selected the wrong man to lead the investigation into the presumed murder of the Fountains. Baca, whose ego equaled or exceeded Garrett's, further proclaimed he knew more about the kidnapping than anyone in the state. Thornton chose to ignore Baca. Garrett also tried hard to ignore the Socorro sheriff, but he was stung by the criticism. As Garrett was settling into his new job and preparing to undertake the investigation the Fountain case demanded but had not yet received, he was immediately visited by a number of citizens who claimed to know who was behind the crime. The name Oliver Lee came up time and again.

Meanwhile, Sheriff Reymond was not up to the pressure being placed upon him to relinquish his office. In response, he told everyone he decided to vacate his position and move to Switzerland. Just as it appeared that things were about to calm down and smooth out, Thornton threw a wrench into the machinery—he summoned the Pinkerton Detective Agency to get involved in the investigation. Pinkerton Operative J.C. Fraser arrived in Santa Fe on March 4, 1897 was briefed by the governor, and then traveled to Las Cruces.

Garrett was perplexed by what he considered an intrusion into his investigation by the Pinkerton operative. Further, Garrett was intimidated by the newcomer; Fraser was highly trained detective and got along well with everyone. Garrett, on the other hand, was untrained, undisciplined, and governed by a huge ego. He was further annoyed when he learned that the governor requested progress reports on the investigation from Fraser and not him.

While Garrett fretted and stewed about his predicament, Fraser was busy working on the Fountain case. He interviewed Major Llewellyn, who informed him of all he knew about Oliver Lee and Albert Fall. When Llewellyn tried to meet with Garrett to compare specific notes on the investigation, Garrett would tell the major that he had already looked into that aspect of the case and that "there was nothing to it." Garrett told Llewellyn that he had already interviewed everyone, but the truth was that Garrett had done little to no investigating at all.

Based on what he had gleaned thus far with his investigation, Fraser recommended indictments be initiated for the arrests of Oliver Lee, Bill McNew, Jim Gilliland, and Bill Carr. Fraser also wanted an indictment against Albert Fall as an accomplice, but was not confident enough that he could prove complicity. When Garrett learned of Fraser's intentions, he confronted him and told him it was a bad idea because of the political situation. He told Fraser that any arrests should not take place until he, Garrett, had been formally appointed sheriff, and until they had accumulated more evidence. Fraser argued that he had enough to develop a strong case for the arrest and prosecution of Lee and company and that all he needed was for Garrett to obtain statements from them. It was clear to Fraser that all Garrett knew about the case was what he had heard from Fountain supporters. He addressed Garrett and related his opinion, which further enraged and distanced him. Garrett informed Fraser that it would be difficult to arrest Lee and his men; they would be hard to find and they were dangerous. Garrett argued for constructing a case against Lee *et al* slowly and carefully. Garrett suggested they isolate either McNew or Gilliland and try to get one or both of them to turn on Lee.

About that time, Albert Fall, good friend to and attorney for Lee, decided that Garrett might possibly be useful to him. He arranged a meeting with Garrett and assured him that he would eventually be named sheriff of Doña Ana County. The ever-conniving Fall convinced the gullible Garrett that he, Fall, was on his side and could play an important and supportive role.

Garrett had his heart set firm on becoming sheriff. During one of his meetings with Fraser, he told the detective that if he were not appointed sheriff or deputy sheriff that he would resign from the investigation altogether. Fraser was concerned that if Garrett were to remove himself from the case, then there would be no one left who could initiate the necessary warrants against Oliver Lee and others.

On March 18, Fraser and Garrett met with Albert Fall and Oliver Lee. Fraser wanted to interview the two men separately but Garrett would have none of it. Fall was the first to arrive at the meeting. He told Fraser that he had never cared for Fountain "any more than he did a snake." He also said that Jack Fountain was accusing him, Fall, of planning the murder. When Fraser asked Fall to account for his time on the afternoon of the disappearance, Fall stated that he had arrived at Las Cruces at eight o'clock in the evening, went to his home, and had supper.

A moment later Oliver Lee entered the room and Fraser turned his attention to him. At the first question, Fall interrupted and told Fraser that he was aware that Lee had been connected to the disappearance of Fountain and of the warrants for his arrest. Fall explained that he had instructed Lee not to talk to anyone relative to where he was on the afternoon in question "or any other day." "When the time comes," said Fall, "I have the papers and witnesses to prove where Oliver Lee was." Lee remained silent.

When the interview was concluded, Fraser invited everyone in attendance to a nearby saloon for drinks and cigars. While Garrett availed himself of the opportunity, Fraser noted that Lee neither drank nor smoked.

On March 19, 1897, District Judge Gordon Bantz declared Numa Reymond, who did not go to Switzerland and remained in Las Cruces, the winner of the disputed sheriff election. The next day, Ascarate moved out of his office. Garrett wasted no time in arranging for a meeting with Reymond. Bypassing all preliminaries, Garrett got straight to the point and asked Reymond when he was going to appoint him chief deputy, and when the entire office of sheriff would eventually be turned over to him. Reymond informed Garrett he had no such plans to do anything of the sort. He further surprised Garrett by telling him that he had appointed Oscar Lohman to the position of chief deputy. Reymond also told Garrett that the best he could do was to hire him as a regular deputy in charge of the Fountain case.

Garrett flew into a rage. He realized that if this were to come to pass, that he would be in a position of having to report to Reymond and

Lohman. Further, if Reymond decided to vacate the position of sheriff, then the politically well-connected Lohman would likely be promoted to the position. Angered, Garrett stomped out of Reymond's office.

Major Llewellyn stepped into the fray. After applying his influence to a number of Las Cruces businessmen, he raised $1,000 that was used to bribe Reymond and Lohman. After receiving his payoff, Lohman announced his resignation and Garrett was appointed to the position of chief deputy. According to some researchers, even more money was raised and passed on to Reymond. Whatever the circumstances, the sheriff resigned his position during the last week of April and Garrett was named the new sheriff of Doña Ana County.

On March 20, Pinkerton detective Fraser, accompanied by Llewellyn, rode to and inspected much of the territory in and around the area where Fountain disappeared. A few people were interviewed but nothing was learned above and beyond what he already knew or suspected. Later when Fraser attempted to communicate with Garrett he was ignored. Fraser returned to the Pinkerton headquarters in Denver on March 25. On April 15, W. B. Sayers, the Pinkerton detective who was to replace Fraser, arrived in Santa Fe for a briefing with Governor Thornton.

Sayers' first move was to interview Slick Miller who was serving time in a New Mexico prison. Miller knew all of the details relative to the first plot to assassinate Fountain. Miller, in fact, had been sentenced by Fountain. Under questioning by Sayers, Miller revealed the 1884 plans by Lee, McNew, and Bill Carr to kill Colonel Fountain. Miller claimed the man in charge of the plot was Ed Brown, a small time cattle rustler from Socorro. Miller told Sayers that the men who killed Fountain were the same ones behind the establishment of the cattlemen's association. After gleaning this information, Sayers decided to offer Brown immunity if he would provide information leading to the arrests and convictions of the Fountain murderers.

Brown was arrested on a charge of rustling. Sayers, accompanied by a handful of local law enforcement officers, tried to intimidate Brown into believing that if he did not provide pertinent information regarding the Fountain case that he would be sent to prison for a long time. Brown refused to be intimidated and denied any knowledge whatsoever of a plot to kill Fountain. He refused to answer questions and had to be released.

Having achieved little to no success with their investigation, the Pinkertons decided to pull out of the Fountain case. Sayers returned to

Denver on May 16, 1898. This left Pat Garrett as the sole investigator.

More time passed and no headway was made relative to the Fountain probe. Garrett explained that he had been so busy with the mundane duties of enforcing the law in Doña Ana County that he had little time for such. In spite of Garrett's investigatory ineptitude, he was awarded the position of United States deputy marshal.

The reason for the appointment lay in immigration difficulties. Around this time, the U. S. government was growing increasingly concerned over the growing smuggling of Chinese laborers into the U.S. from across the Mexican border. Hundreds of Chinese had been employed as laborers during the construction of over 1,000 miles of railway throughout Mexico. The Asians were often subjected to violent discrimination. With much of the railroad work completed, the Chinese looked north toward the Rio Grande, perceiving that life would be much better for them in the United States.

In 1882, the U. S. passed the Chinese Exclusion Act, the first American law restricting immigration based on race and/or ethnicity. The rationale, according to Nancy Davis of the National Museum of American History, was that the Chinese were taking jobs away from Americans, but the truth was that raging xenophobia prompted the bill. (The bill was finally repealed only in 1943 in order to improve relations with China, and in 2011 and 2012, the Senate and the House of Representatives passed a resolution apologizing for the clearly racist exclusion act.)

Garrett's appointment was related to facilitating the investigation of any migrant activity in his jurisdiction. In addition, Garrett, who was always broke, needed the money.

Pat Garrett

22
LEE-GARRETT CONFRONTATION

Two years passed with no progress made on the Fountain case. Governor Thornton served out his term and the new reigning bureaucrat was Miguel Otero. Otero, along with others, had heard rumors that Fountain was not dead at all, that he had been seen in Texas, Cuba, Mexico, and even Hawaii. The cause of his disappearance, according to the gossip, was related to domestic troubles, boredom, or pursuing some adventure or another. The rumors, many were convinced, were generated by Albert Fall.

Otero was interested in the Fountain matter and expressed disappointment in the way the case had been handled thus far by Garrett. Otero let Garrett know that he wanted some action, some results. Concerned that he might be removed from his position as sheriff of Doña Ana County, Garrett decided to undertake some activity; he determined to seek indictments. The grand jury was set to meet on April 1, and Garrett served notice on prospective jurors in Tularosa.

While he was in town, Garrett stopped at Tipton's Saloon and General Store and was surprised to run into Albert Fall, Oliver Lee, District Clerk George Curry, and Tobe Tipton, all engaged in a poker game. When Tipton vacated his seat to attend to some business, Garrett took it.

What followed was a seventy-hour poker game. During the contest, Lee and Garrett verbally sparred with one another. Both men carried revolvers, and neither was inclined to turn his back on the other. At one point, George Curry spoke up and addressed Garrett, telling him that he had heard that someone sitting at the table was to be indicted for murdering the Fountains. Curry further stated that whoever it was would likely hire a lawyer, the very one that was sitting across the table from Garrett.

Tipton later stated that, "There was more dynamite gathered around that poker table than could be found in any other town in New Mexico. There we were, sitting on a powder keg, and Curry deliberately struck a match."

Following Curry's comment, Lee told Garrett that if he planned on serving papers on him that he knew where to find him. Garrett said if he intended to serve such papers that he would send them or have them delivered by Curry. The game finally broke up and Garrett returned to Las Cruces.

The next day, Lee traveled to Las Cruces to see what action the grand jury had taken. He learned that the jury had met and adjourned without ever having discussed him or the Fountains. Lee found this odd, given that Garrett claimed to be soliciting jurors to issue indictments. Lee was beginning to think he had been outsmarted by the sheriff. Garrett knew everyone was certain that the grand jury would issue indictments. If none were handed down, the sheriff was convinced that the result would be confusion on the part of Lee. Garrett believed that the best time to strike was when there was confusion. While pondering this situation, Lee dropped a bundle of clothes off at Henry Stoes' cleaning establishment and purchased a train ticket to El Paso.

Lee had barely departed town when Garrett approached Judge Frank Parker, presented the necessary papers, and requested bench warrants for Lee, McNew, Gilliland, and Bill Carr. Garrett's deposition concluded with the sentence, "Oliver Lee, William McNew, and James Gilliland are the parties who murdered Colonel Albert J. Fountain and his son, Henry Fountain." A second affidavit, signed by Thomas Brannigan and W. H. H. Llewellyn, explained the activities of the search party that went out on February 2 and found tracks pointing to "one Oliver Lee, William McNew, one Carr, and one Gilliland." Parker issued the warrants.

Later when Garrett was asked why he had Judge Parker issue the warrants when the grand jury had been assembled for the handling of the matter, he replied that the defendants' attorneys "had access to the grand jury room and had they been indicted, I'm satisfied the prisoners would have known it before the officers."

While Garrett now had the warrants he needed, he made no attempt to serve them. Two days later when Lee returned from El Paso, he went to Stoes' cleaning establishment to pick up his clothes and learned about the warrants. Lee told Stoes, "Pat Garrett will shoot me in the back if he ever arrests me, and will claim it was self defense. I won't let them take me that way." Lee rode back to his ranch.

People who claimed to be in the know stated that Garrett was afraid of Lee, afraid to try to arrest him on even terms. Garrett, for his part, simply stated that he was waiting to arrest Lee on his own terms.

On April 3, 1897, Carr and McNew were arrested. A posse of eight men deputized by Garrett rode to Lee's ranch to serve warrants. Perhaps it is telling that Garrett was not among them. Lee ignored the posse even though they brought a note from Albert Fall informing Lee that he was wanted in town. Lee stood on the porch of his ranch house and glared at the posse members for a moment, then stepped inside his house and slammed the door. The posse men were clearly intimidated by Lee, a man known to be fearless and to have killed others. They sat their horses and discussed what their next move should be when Tom Tucker stepped outside the house and told the posse men that Lee was not at home. One of the posse members suggested they enter the house and arrest Lee, but the rest felt they should depart for Las Cruces immediately. The deputies returned to town without having served the warrants.

The following day, Lee was back in El Paso. He sent word that if the court would determine a reasonable bond for him, that he would travel to Las Cruces and turn himself in. According to the June 7, 1890, issue of the El Paso *Daily Herald*, Lee stated that he did not wish to be taken to Las Cruces and kept in a jail "for an indefinite period without trial."

Lee was certain that Garrett did not have enough evidence to convict him of anything. Lee was also certain that he intimidated Garrett and kept him off-balance. Garrett was well aware that Lee was regarded as a powerful rancher and was well respected politically. Garrett, on the other hand, had made little to no progress on the Fountain investigation in the two years he had been in office, and was stung by the ongoing criticism of the governor.

On April 10, Carr and McNew were brought before Judge Parker. The court was to determine whether or not there was enough evidence to try the two men for the murder of Fountain. Albert Fall jumped into the middle of the affair. Fall was determined to convince the prosecution that they did not have a sufficient case against against the two prisoners. For assistance, Fall summoned Judge H. L. Warren from Albuquerque, an experienced trial lawyer as well as the district attorney. He also called upon Judge Harry Daugherty from Socorro to assist him. Daugherty had been following the ongoing Fountain investigation and was so fascinated by it, along with the alleged participants, that he resigned his office to become involved.

Lee was concerned that his cowhands Carr and McNew would crumble under Garrett's interrogation and talk too much. Lee also fretted that Garrett might offer the two men a deal wherein they would be set free if they testified against him.

The preliminary trial went on for six days. Witnesses who had experience with, or a relationship with, Fountain's activities were brought in to testify. The most powerful testimony was that of Jack Maxwell. Maxwell testified that Lee, Gilliland, and McNew had not been at the ranch on the day of the Fountain murder, that they had arrived that night on worn out horses and appeared to be concerned and preoccupied about something. The prosecution was feeling good about Maxwell's testimony up until it was time for Albert Fall to question him.

By the time Fall got finished with Maxwell, it seemed as though the young man wasn't certain of anything. Fall tricked him into contradicting himself on several points, and by the time he was excused, Maxwell turned out to be a better witness for the defense than for the prosecution.

Garrett, who should have known better, paraded one witness after another before the court, each of them providing nothing of substance in the way of evidence or pertinent testimony and essentially wasting the prosecution's time. As if things were not going bad enough for the prosecution, it was discovered that much of the evidence that had been found at the site of the presumed Fountain abduction and elsewhere along the pursuit route had vanished.

On the final day of the preliminary trial, Maxwell was called back to the stand. There, Fall got him to admit that he had been promised a share of the $10,000 reward for the killers of Fountain. Then, as it was discovered that Pat Garrett had made an agreement with Maxwell promising him $2,000 if his testimony led to the conviction of Lee, Gilliland, and McNew. Fall made certain everyone understood that Sheriff Garrett was trying to purchase evidence.

By the time the proceedings were over, Fall moved that the prisoners be released on the basis of insufficient evidence. Parker agreed that he did not have enough on Carr to hold him any longer. As for McNew, he was sent back to the jail and denied bond. McNew remained in jail for more than a year.

Oliver Lee followed the proceedings from a distance. He was afraid that he would wind up like McNew—held in jail for a long period of time as the case progressed. He grew wary and made himself scarce. Then, he learned that a newly formed posse was after him. This one was composed in large part of former members of the Republican militia company and was led by territorial militia captain Eugene Van Patten. His orders were to get Oliver Lee.

23
SHOOTOUT AT WILDY WELL

Pat Garrett's reputation as a fearless and heroic lawman was dimming fast. Whatever notoriety and prestige had once been attached to Garrett had long since faded, and had even grown tarnished. People have short memories, and their recollections of the days of Billy the Kid's rustling activities and subsequent pursuit by Garrett, if they had any at all, were by now a generation old. In addition, Garrett's inability to make any progress on the Fountain case left the impression among many that he was little more than a political appointee and lacked competence.

Garrett spent a good deal of his time in the office of sheriff of Doña Ana County trying to advance his cause with politicians and successful businessmen. He rarely met and mingled with the majority of the county's citizens and few of them cared anything at all for him. Months had passed since swearing out indictments for Lee and Gilliland, and yet the two men were still at large. Virtually everyone in the county knew exactly where Lee and Gilliland were, but the consensus of most of the population was that Garrett was afraid of meeting up and tangling with Oliver Lee.

Garrett needed to do something to salvage his position, to change the momentum, and most importantly to him, to reposition himself in the eyes of his voters. An opportunity to do so was on the horizon, an opportunity to put to rest all of the concerns related to his abilities as a law enforcement officer. As with many opportunities that Garrett had presented to him during his lifetime, he was to bungle this one.

While Garrett was pondering his next actions, Albert Fall joined the U. S. Army, as he stated, to fight the Spanish in Cuba. While Fall's cronies praised his dedication and loyalty, it is more likely that the politician wanted to add such service to his resumé, an important consideration for many voters. As it turned out, Fall never set foot in Cuba. He was assigned to a military legal office and never left the U. S. Additionally, Fall was not in the least concerned about leaving his clients Oliver Lee, Jim Gilliland, and Bill McNew. Fall's opinion of these men was much higher than his opinion of Garrett, and he felt certain they could elude or outwit the bumbling sheriff.

Lee and Gilliland rarely went to the Dog Canyon ranch house, which they suspected was being watched. Print Rhode and W. W. Cox, both men brothers-in-law to Lee, provided the fugitives with supplies and fresh horses when needed. Rhode and Cox both despised Garrett.

On July 11, 1898, cattle branding was taking place on the Cox Ranch in the Organ Mountains. Among those helping with the branding were Lee and Gilliland. Lee was also interested in Cox's sister-in-law, Winnie Rhode. Lee was thirty-two years old, had been shy and reserved for most of his life, particularly around women, but was attracted to Winnie enough to overcome his shyness.

As the branding progressed, two of Garrett's deputies who were on the lookout for Lee and Gilliland—José Espalin and Clint Llewellyn—rode up to Cox's corral and found the two men there. Rather than the situation becoming a confrontation, the four men, each of whom knew one another, spent several minutes in conversation. During their chat, Lee mentioned that he and Gilliland were planning to ride over to the Wildy Well cabin where they would spend the night. As Espalin and Llewellyn were preparing to ride away, the former approached Lee and warned him that Garrett was hunting for him. After saying their goodbyes, the two deputies rode straight to Garrett and informed him of Lee's plans.

Garrett went to work putting together a posse. It included Espalin, Llewellyn, Ben Williams, and Kent Kearney. Kearney seemed an unlikely choice for a posse member. He was employed as a school teacher and possessed no experience whatsoever with law enforcement or firearms. Just before sunset, Garrett led the posse out onto the road to Lee's Wildy Well ranch, forty miles away. By four o'clock in the morning, the posse was within one mile of the ranch. Here, they dismounted, tied off their horses, and proceeded on foot to the cabin.

For a century, writers and historians have referred to this location as Wildy Well, and since that has become the name most commonly used and seen, it will be the one applied here. It was originally designated as Wilde's Well, named after rancher John H. Wilde. The name has gone through an evolution from Wilde's Well to Wildey's Well to Wildy Well.

While Lee and Gilliland were on the run, the cabin at the Wildy Well portion of the ranch was occupied by James and Mary Madison and their children. The Madison's were employed by Lee and they watched over his cattle operation there. Lee and Gilliland, along with two of Lee's ranch hands including his nephew, Todd Bailey, were asleep on the flat roof that night.

The cabin was constructed of adobe. Attached to it was a roofed wagon port. The roof of the port was a few feet lower than that of the cabin. Nearby were a pump house, a large water tank, a corral, and an assortment of outbuildings scattered about. On approaching the cabin, Garrett spotted two horses in the corral belonging to Lee and Gilliland. In silence, the sheriff led his men toward the house.

On reaching the porch, Garrett, revolver in hand, stepped up onto it, approached the front door, and put his ear to it. He heard snoring. He tried the door latch and found it unlocked. Standing next to Garrett was Kearney. The sheriff indicated he wanted Kearney to accompany him inside. A second later, Garrett pushed the door opened, stepped inside, and jammed his handgun into the first sleeper he encountered, shouting that everyone was under arrest.

The person in the bed lurched to a seated position and screamed. To Garrett's dismay, it was Mary Madison. Within seconds, the remainder of the cabin's occupants—James Madison, the two children, and a man named McVey—were awake and appearing confused. Garrett demanded to know where Lee and Gilliland were but received no answer. Now, he realized, he would have to search for his quarry.

As Garrett and the deputies searched outbuildings, the sheriff happened to glance back toward the cabin and noticed that McVey appeared to be trying to communicate with someone on the roof. Garrett noted that the adobe walls of the cabin projected about two feet above the level of the roof to form a parapet, and realized immediately that it served as a substantial defensive position. Garrett searched for and found a ladder, carried it to the house, and leaned it against one wall. He then ordered McVey to climb the ladder and instruct the men on the roof to surrender and climb down. McVey refused. Garrett turned to Madison and related the same order, but Madison likewise refused.

According to Garrett, he told Ben Williams to take a position behind the water tank. He told Llewellyn to move the Madison family and McVey back into the house and stand guard over them. Garrett moved the ladder to the wagon port and he, Espalin, and Kearney climbed to its roof. From their position, they could just barely see a portion of the cabin roof but spotted no one. Espalin found a smaller ladder and handed it up to Garrett who placed it against the wall of the house. Kearney stepped up a couple of rungs so he could get a better view, and at the same time, according to Garrett, he yelled for whoever was on the roof to surrender.

When interviewed later, Oliver Lee stated that this was not true, that the call to surrender came only after Garrett and the deputies started shooting. Lee stated that he "was asleep when fired upon." It is difficult to believe that the men on the roof—four of them—could have remained asleep with all of the activity taking place below in the house and yard, as well as the screaming of Mary Madison. Lee claimed, "Kearney fired twice and Garrett also fired before I fired. I heard no commands of 'hands-up,' but Garrett was talking while shooting." In addition to Lee, Gilliland and the two ranch hands, including Todd Bailey, returned fire. As far as is known, this is the first time Garrett encountered Todd Bailey. It would not be the last.

Two of Garrett's bullets struck the roof close to Lee, scattering gravel, dirt, and twigs. Garrett dropped down from his position just as Lee returned fire. As Lee fired, so did one of his cowhands, the bullet striking Kearney in the groin. The deputy fell from the ladder, rolled across the wagon port roof, and tumbled down to the ground.

Concerned that he might be the next to get shot, Garrett jumped from the port roof and sought cover inside one of the nearby outbuildings. He never stopped to examine the condition of Kearney. Espalin likewise fled from the roof, but as he moved away from the scene, the shooting by Lee and his men forced him to a position up against the wall of the house. From the outbuilding in which he was hiding, Garrett heard Madison yelling at him that he wanted to take his family to the root cellar in order to get them out of the line of fire. Garrett told him to go ahead. In his hurry, Madison forgot his daughter, who was left inside the house.

From his position beneath the water tank, Ben Williams shot at the gunfire flashes he spotted from the roof. His attack was answered immediately; several bullets punctured the tank, spilling water onto the deputy. Unable to flee, he was forced to remain under the flow of water in the freezing weather. This left Garrett as the only member of the posse who was in a position to effectively fight Lee and his cowhands.

According to R. L. Madison, the son of James Madison, Lee called

Garrett a bastard and scorned the lawman for shooting at him and his men at the same time he was calling for surrender. Garrett yelled back at Lee to lay down his arms and give up, but the rancher refused, stating that he was convinced Garrett would kill him if he did.

According to Buck Bailey, the grandson of Todd Bailey, Lee ordered all of the lawmen to drop their guns. Garrett replied that he was afraid to do so, afraid that he would be killed. Lee told Garrett that he was a man of his word and that if he and his deputies dropped their weapons he would let them ride out. Garrett finally agreed.

Leaving the outbuilding, Garrett's path took him by the mortally wounded Kearney. He could see that the young man was in severe pain and unlikely to live. From the roof of the house, Lee, in strong terms, repeated his order to Garrett to ride away.

Garrett, Williams, and Espalin rode several miles to a location called Turquoise Siding where they encountered a railroad section line crew. Garrett talked some of the men into taking a wagon to Wildy Well and retrieving Kearney. When the railroad crew arrived later, they found Lee and his men sitting with the badly wounded Kearney, talking to him and attempting to make him comfortable. Kearney was loaded into the wagon and the workers drove him back to Turquoise Siding where Garrett waited. The sheriff had Kearney loaded onto a train and carried to Alamogordo. There, he was removed and placed in another wagon which carried him to La Luz. Kearney died the following day.

It did not take long for word of Garrett's humiliating defeat at the hands of Oliver Lee to make the rounds of the Tularosa Basin. Garrett went to Wildy Well feeling as though he had the element of surprise on his side. In turn, he had been forced to surrender, leave his weapons at the site, lose a deputy to gunfire, and chased away. The man he went to arrest embarrassed the sheriff as he had never been before, Garrett's mission was a failure, and the two fugitives were still at large.

It was not long before another indictment was handed down from the grand jury, this one charging Oliver Lee and Jim Gilliland with the murder of Deputy Kerney. With this new charge against him, Lee decided the only thing for him to do was to make himself scarce. He turned the operation of his ranch over to some of his trusted cowhands and he, along with Gilliland, rode off into the mountains to hide out for a time.

W. W. Cox

24
FUGITIVES

Oliver Lee and Jim Gilliland were on the run. Wanted for the killing of Albert Jennings Fountain, Henry Fountain, and Deputy Ken Kearney, Lee decided it was best that the two of them stay as far away from Pat Garrett as possible until arrangements could be made that would offer protection. Lee was convinced that Garrett cared little about bringing him in alive. He was convinced that Garrett wanted to kill him, and he depended on his friend and attorney Albert Fall to provide for his safety.

Lee was generally well liked throughout the area, had friends and supporters among the community of small ranchers scattered throughout the Tularosa Basin and beyond, and he was welcome on their property anytime. One of those friends was Charley Graham who operated a ranch north of Las Cruces on the edge of the *Jornada del Muerto.* The *Jornada del Muerto* translates to "The Journey of Death," and refers to a vast expanse of waterless desert and scrub landscape located between the Rio Grande and the San Andres and Oscura mountain ranges where many travelers and migrants lost their lives to thirst, heat, or Indian attack.

Lee and Gilliland would drop in on Graham from time to time to replenish supplies and provisions. When it as known that Garrett was in the area searching for the fugitives, Graham would carry supplies out to where Lee and Gilliland were camped. During this time, Lee and Gilliland grew beards.

On one occasion, Lee encountered Garrett on a road, the two men traveling in opposite directions. By this time, Lee had grown a long beard and he wore dirty, ragged clothes. To Garrett, he appeared to be just another drifter.

Another of Lee's friends was Eugene Manlove Rhodes who owned a ranch in the San Andres Mountains. It is believed that Lee and Gilliland spent most of their time on the dodge with Rhodes.

Rhodes was a fascinating figure. Originally from Nebraska, he moved with his parents to New Mexico in 1881. There he spent twenty-five years as a cowhand and rancher. Rhodes was an unlikely cow man and a confidant to outlaws. He has been described as smaller than average and had a speech impediment. Lee and Gilliland were not the first men on the run to whom Rhodes provided shelter. He was known to be sympathetic to a number of law breakers, often providing sanctuary. One of his most colorful guests was the noted train robber, Thomas "Black Jack" Ketchum. Rhodes eventually left his ranch for New York and became a nationally famous writer of a number of novels. He also wrote for newspapers and magazines.

While staying with Rhodes, Lee wrote and sent letters to the Las Cruces *Independent Democrat* wherein he provided an explanation for his flight from Garrett and his reasons for not surrendering to him. He wrote that Garrett "repeatedly and publicly threatened to kill him."

In October 1898, Lee shaved his beard and made his way to San Antonio, Texas. He was joined by Winnie Rhode, rancher W. W. Cox's sister-in-law. There, the two were married in the home of Jim Hester, a veteran of the famous Sutton-Taylor Feud in Texas two decades earlier. At this point, all traces of Oliver Lee have been impossible to follow, then and now. What is known, however, is that in March 1899 he was back in the San Andres Mountains. While Winnie lived at the ranch, Lee and Gilliland remained in hiding and waited for Albert Fall's return from his stint in the military. Lee regrew his beard.

During the two years that Pat Garrett had been in charge of the Fountain investigation, little to nothing had been accomplished save for the arrest of Bill McNew. This, however, proved insignificant, since McNew provided no pertinent information whatsoever. Garrett's hopes that McNew would break down and incriminate Lee were dashed. Furthermore, Garrett was receiving pressure from Governor Otero as well as the citizens of New Mexico. Garrett assured them all that he was indeed active in the investigation, and that positive results were forthcoming.

Albert Fall finally returned to Las Cruces following his time in the military, and he set his sights on paving the way for Lee and Gilliland to turn themselves in with a guarantee of safety. Meanwhile, Gilliland was proving to be somewhat of a liability. Often described as a boastful man, he took pleasure in bragging to friends about his role in the killing of Fountain and his son. Fall was concerned that Gilliland was talking too much. Furthermore, Fall was afraid that if Gilliland were arrested by Garrett, that he would reveal more than what the lawyer and Lee wanted the sheriff to know, thus creating problems for the courtroom defense. Fall cautioned Gilliland to keep his mouth shut.

It is generally believed that Fall met with Oliver Lee during the latter's time in hiding. It was known that Fall was debating different strategies and no doubt would have conferred with Lee about them. One strategy was for Lee to continue to remain in hiding since the maladroit Garrett was not able to find him. Another was to have Lee surrender to Garrett, a decision fraught with potentially negative consequences for Lee. The third strategy was to arrange to have Lee and Gilliland surrender to law enforcement authorities outside of Garrett's jurisdiction. As Fall pondered these moves, he decided that the third strategy held the most promise. His decision was to set in motion the creation of a new county for the Territory of New Mexico. He lost no time in going to work on his scheme.

Fall contacted W. A. Hawkins, an attorney for the El Paso and Northeastern Railroad. Hawkins had expressed a desire to see a new county formed but for different reasons. The EP & N had made an earlier arrangement with Oliver Lee. Lee sold a significant portion of his Dog Canyon Ranch to the railroad company in 1897 for $5,000. By 1898, the railroad was running its trains through this stretch of land from El Paso to Alamogordo. In addition, an agreement was made to construct a system of canals across Lee's ranch to deliver water from the Sacramento Mountains to several railroad stations along the route. The geography involved in all of this was located in Doña Ana County where Pat Garrett was sheriff.

The railroad representatives were concerned that Doña Ana County officials manifested little interest in and offered no assistance toward the operations of the railroad. They failed to provide and maintain roads, and communication lines were insufficient to non-existent. The railroad company argued for a new county staffed with interested and helpful officials. They also argued that the county seat should be Alamogordo. Albert Fall took on the responsibility of petitioning for a new county as long as it was agreed that the western boundary would extend beyond the San Andres Mountains. If this could be accomplished, the new county would thus contain the site of the alleged Fountain murder and assume legal jurisdiction, therefore removing Doña Ana County and its officials from jurisdiction.

Republican Senator Thomas Catron, who did not care for Fall, was opposed to the recommendation. Even Governor Otero, who cared little for Catron, was opposed to the idea. Both Catron and Otero were convinced that Oliver Lee was behind the killing of Fountain and were not inclined to do anything that would hamper his arrest and prosecution.

A careful study of New Mexico politics and personalities would convince anyone that Fall and Hawkins were considerably more intelligent and clever than the politicians Catron and Otero. Knowing how much Otero was motivated by ego, Fall proposed that the new county be named after him. It took only a few minutes for Otero to change his mind and declare that the new county was a good idea. Otero County was officially recognized on January 30, 1899. Not long afterward, George Curry was named county sheriff.

With the new county in place, events were set in motion for Lee and Gilliland to surrender. The arrangement was handled by Eugene Manlove Rhodes. Rhodes contacted Otero County Sheriff Curry and informed him that the two fugitives would be brought in under two conditions: (1) They would not be placed in the Doña Ana County jail, and (2) they would not be turned over to Sheriff Pat Garrett. Curry immediately contacted Governor Otero for instructions on how to respond. Otero said the conditions could be met.

It was agreed that Lee and Gilliland would be taken to Las Cruces to surrender to Judge Frank Parker. On March 14, 1899, Lee and Gilliland, both still wearing beards and tattered clothes, were placed aboard a train a Las Cruces-bound train at Socorro and accompanied by Rhodes. Unknown to the three of them, Garrett was on the same train. Garrett, accompanied by his old friend Texas Ranger Captain John Hughes, was transporting a prisoner from Santa Fe to El Paso.

Garrett and Hughes entered the smoking car where Lee and Gilliland were seated. For several minutes, Hughes thumbed through a magazine within an arm's length of Gilliland. Garrett walked down the aisle and paused next to the seat occupied by Lee. He bent down and looked past him out the window for a full minute. Presently Garrett and Hughes departed the car.

According to writer W. H. Hutchinson, there is little agreement among historians as to whether or not Garrett recognized Lee. Gilliland was convinced that he did, and he implied that Garrett was too frightened of Lee to make an arrest, or even say anything. It is inconceivable that the beard worn by Lee and blue eyeglasses worn by Gilliland were enough to fool Garrett, a long-time lawman who had been close to both men on several occasions. Garrett once sat at a poker table in Tipton's Store with fellow participant Lee for seventy hours and had met with him on at least two other occasions.

When the train arrived at Las Cruces, Rhodes escorted Lee and Gilliland to the home of Judge Parker where they formally surrendered. Because the construction of the Alamogordo jail had not been completed, the two prisoners were installed in the Las Cruces County jail despite the earlier agreement not to do so. A short time later, Parker agreed to have the two prisoners placed under the authority of Socorro County Sheriff C. F. Blackington and housed in the Socorro County jail. Several days later when the construction of the Otero County jail had been completed, Lee and Gilliland were transferred back to El Paso where they were to be put aboard an EP & N train for Alamogordo, the county seat.

Sheriff Blackington met the two men at the El Paso station and was to escort them to Alamogordo. He nevertheless left Lee and Gilliland waiting at the El Paso train station. Blackington, who arrived at El Paso to escort the prisoners, stepped down the block to a tavern for a few drinks. In a remarkably short time, Blackington became drunk and unruly and was arrested by El Paso Constable Mannen Clements. Clements did not believe the sheriff's story that he was on official business and was escorting dangerous criminals. Clements placed him in jail.

Somehow, Lee discerned what had occurred. He walked over to the jail and identified Blackington for Clements who released him. An hour later, Lee, Gilliland, and Blackington were on their way to Alamogordo.

Eugene Manlove Rhodes

25
MOVING TOWARD A TRIAL

After remaining fugitives for three years and living in hiding, Oliver Lee, along with his two ranch hands Jim Gilliland and Bill McNew, were charged with, and arrested for, the murder of Albert Jennings Fountain and his eight-year-old son, Henry. The next item on the legal agenda was to schedule a trial for the three men. At this time, however, no bodies had been found.

It has been oft-stated by lawmen, courtroom reporters, and students of the legal system that once a case has been brought into court, it matters not whether the charged person was guilty or not, but who had the best lawyer. The prosecution in this case was to be handled by District Attorney R. P. Barnes of Silver City, William Burr Childers of Albuquerque, and Thomas Benton Catron of Santa Fe. The defense was represented by Harvey B. Ferguson of Albuquerque, Harry M. Daugherty of Socorro, and a man who was generally feared by the prosecution—Albert B. Fall.

Oliver Lee had many supporters, many friends. Sides were taken in large part related to whatever political party one belonged to, and the looming trial was beginning to look like a battle between Republicans, represented by Barnes, Catron, and Childers, and Democrats represented by Oliver Lee and Albert Fall. Most of the cattlemen in the Tularosa Basin, and there were many, were on Lee's side, he being one of them and admired by most. Lee's success in evading pursuit for years and flaunting the law impressed others, many of whom felt they were themselves victims of the political and legal systems. As the days passed and moved toward a trial date, public opinion seemed to be favoring Oliver Lee.

Researcher and author C. L. Sonnichsen opined that:

> Colonel Fountain...was no more than a name to people who had not known him. Nobody seemed interested anymore in dragging the murderers, whoever they were, to justice, for by this time the Fountain case was just an excuse for bringing a great political feud to a showdown. The Democrats, because they hated Catron and the Santa Fe ring, were automatically convinced of the innocence of Oliver Lee *et al.* Every good Republican was just as certain that he was guilty as hell.

For sheer drama, the case could not have been scripted better. It came to court on three different occasions. The prosecution wanted the trail to be held in Las Cruces, but it was argued by Fall that since that was Fountain's hometown, most of the jurors would be prejudiced. The prosecution objected, but eventually caved in. New Mexico residents, as well as many others throughout the Southwest, looked on with interest. The first court session amounted to little. On March 25, 1899, Judge Parker decided that for two of the three indictments on which the accused were to be tried, the trial was to take place at Silver City. There, the hearing was held on the third Monday in April. The prosecution was anxious to try Oliver Lee first and separate from the other two prisoners. The prosecution feared that if they tried either Gilliland or McNew first, that much of their strategy and evidence would be revealed, and anticipated that the clever and devious Albert Fall would use their methods against them when it came time to defend Lee.

The judge, however, declared that McNew should be tried first. Rather than expose any part of their plan, the prosecution decided to release McNew. Further, the first two indictments were dropped. The remaining indictment—the charge of murdering young Henry Fountain—was then scheduled to be heard the following month at the courthouse in Hillsboro, New Mexico, a tiny mining town located on the eastern slope of the Black Range and some forty miles east of Silver City.

Hillsboro seemed at first like an odd choice as a setting for this event, but most were agreed that the town offered the best opportunity to assemble an impartial jury. Many residing in the town were unaware of the disappearance of Colonel Fountain and Garrett's fruitless efforts to locate and arrest the suspects.

Hillsboro was a small yet picturesque town in the wooded foothills of the Black Range and had a population of just under two hundred residents. Water was plentiful in this part of the state, and the Middle Percha Creek wound its way through the town. In Hillsboro could be found three saloons, the Union Hotel, stores, houses, a jail, a schoolhouse, and, of course, the courthouse. Money from the silver mines and the ore processing operation were the principal sources of income for residents.

Tall, thick cottonwoods grew along the banks of the stream, and rich garden plots had been planted along the fertile flood plain. To the north of town was located a large smelter. The only access and egress to the town was an east-west road that accommodated travelers on horseback and in wagons and stagecoaches. There was no railroad, and until the occasion of the trial of Oliver Lee, there were no telegraph lines.

With his prominence as a southern New Mexico cattleman, as well as his successful evasion of Pat Garrett, Oliver Lee had by now become somewhat of a celebrity. When he arrived in El Paso from Silver City, dozens of the curious were at the station to greet him, to look upon him. Smiling, the charming Lee went into the crowd and shook hands with everyone.

At the station, a newspaper reporter approached Lee and asked him if the rumor that the skeleton of Henry Fountain had been found and that the prosecution was ready to produce Colonel Fountain's bones as well was true. Lee replied:

> No. There is nothing to it that I know of. Fountain may be dead, but we don't have to prove that he is alive to clear ourselves. The prosecution must prove that he is dead and that we killed him, and that cannot be proved. It will be impossible for them to secure a conviction."

It should be noted that Lee did not state his innocence, only that he could not be convicted.

The pending trial at Hillsboro was becoming a major event. Spectators traveled from miles away to attend the proceedings, to witness the skirmish between the two cadres of lawyers. More people arrived than the town was able to accommodate. The Union Hotel had less than twenty rooms. In addition to the judges, the prosecution, the defense, the defendants, and the witnesses, the number of people scheduled to be in the courtroom during the trial numbered close to one hundred. The problem was solved as a result of the establishment of a tent city on the north side of town for the prosecution, and another on the south side of town for the defense. The southern encampment was named the Oliver Lee Camp. Both camps boasted chuck wagons to feed the inhabitants. Each one also had a number of armed guards. Both camps, as well as campsites for the numerous onlookers that stretched across the neighboring hillsides, filled the town to overflowing several days before the trial was to begin. Western Union ran a telegraph line from Lake Valley to Hillsboro.

More people were arriving, among them reporters for area newspapers as well as representatives from the Associated Press and the Hearst news empire. Jack Fountain, a witness for the prosecution, had ridden a stagecoach from Colorado where he had been employed. On arriving, Fall had Fountain escorted to the office of Judge Parker where the lawyer demanded that he be placed under a peace bond. Fall stated that the "defendants and the defense witnesses were in fear of their lives" from Jack Fountain.

When Parker asked Fountain to respond to the request, he said he had no intentions of killing anyone, "though they deserve killing." He then told Parker that "if my father's bones were ever found and identified, and I think I know how to identify them positively, there is one man I would kill myself." When Parker asked him to identify that man, Fountain said, "Albert Bacon Fall." Parker placed Fountain under a $500 peace bond.

A short time later, Catron, Barnes, and Childers of the prosecution team arrived. Two members of the defense team—Daugherty and Ferguson—joined Fall. The trial, in the minds of many onlookers, was shaping up more to be a duel between Catron and Fall.

Catron was not well liked among most people in attendance. It was known that he was affiliated with the Santa Fe Ring, which author Robert M. Utley described as "a band of shrewd lawyers and businessmen [who] made up a loose cabal of opportunists." Members of the ring, according to Utley, "enjoyed modest bonanzas by trafficking in old Spanish land grants, the public domain, and contracts for supporting the territory's huge federal establishment, especially Indian agencies and army forts." The name Catron, according to author Leon Metz, was synonymous with political corruption.

In appearance, Catron was markedly different from the blue-collar residents of Hillsboro and was not well received. He has been described as a "soft, portly man who likely never experienced hard work of any kind... and was perceived as making his living by arranging for taxes on those who did."

By contrast, Albert Fall appealed to the Hillsboro citizens. Where Catron was aloof, Fall was approachable, stopping often to visit with citizens and speak with newspaper reporters. While Catron surrounded himself with his well-dressed and somewhat elegant coterie, Fall was shaking hands, slapping backs, and kissing babies. The shrewd Fall characterized the upcoming contest in the courtroom as a fight between the working class represented by ranchers and farmers and miners just scraping by against the wealthy, the major landowners, and the elite. The lines were drawn, and Fall carefully constructed for himself the image of a giant-killer, and his enemy was the evil power that wielded a heavy hand against the middle and lower class residents of the region.

So caught up were the citizens in Fall's rhetoric that when Pat Garrett arrived in town, he was ignored. Though he had once attained a level of prominence and was a major figure in the upcoming trial, he was provided little to no consideration by the masses.

While Garrett's arrival went largely unnoticed or disregarded, that of Oliver Lee was a highlight for Hillsobro residents. Lee and Gilliland were immediately surrounded by friends and well-wishers and treated as celebrities. Like Fall, they mingled easily with the citizenry, shaking hands and accepting good wishes. Oliver Lee appeared to be having a good time. Arriving with Lee were three of his ranch hands, including his nephew, Todd Bailey. These three were in Hillsboro in the role of bodyguards

With Fall's help, Lee was being portrayed as a Robin Hood-type individual who fought for the little people against the power represented by the likes of Pat Garrett and Thomas Catron. Catron and his people noticed this, and saw how the people were responding to it, and he and his team grew concerned.

The stage was set, and the drama was about to begin.

26
THE TRIAL

The processes relating to the trial of Oliver Lee and Jim Gilliland began on May 25, 1899. The two men were charged with the murder of Henry Fountain. Charges related to the deaths of Colonel Fountain and Deputy Kearney were to be filed at a later date. Jury selection took place between May 25 and May 27. Several of the jurors selected were Mexicans and had little facility with the English language. As a result, an interpreter was enlisted to translate testimony and arguments.

Even as jury selection was under way, Catron and his team looked on and began to feel that their chances for success were diminishing. Key witnesses for the prosecution failed to show up. Three Mexicans who claimed they saw Lee, McNew, and Gilliland ride from the murder scene with a body tied to their horses were nowhere to be found. Jack Maxwell was not present and had to be retrieved from White Oaks by Garrett.

On May 29, the trial officially got under way. As courtroom spectators filed in, Todd Bailey took a position near the front and to one side of the courtroom. A second Lee ranch hand took a similar position on the other side, and a third employee sat in the back. Each of the cowhands carried shotguns and revolvers rolled up in their saddle slickers, long waterproof canvas riding coats.

The first person called by the prosecution was New Mexico Governor Thornton. He testified that he had visited the alleged murder site and a short time afterward offered a reward for the killers. The second witness was Theodore Heman who was there to provide motive. Heman stated that, as foreman of the Lincoln County Grand Jury in 1896, he testified to the cattle rustling indictments handed down against Oliver Lee and Bill McNew. Next, mail carrier Barela related his visit with Colonel Fountain on the road to Las Cruces just prior to his disappearance.

Jack Maxwell was sworn in, and the prosecution was hoping his testimony would be the beginning of the end for Oliver Lee. After he was sworn in, Maxwell stated that he had forgotten his earlier testimony wherein he stated that he was staying at the Dog Canyon ranch house when Lee, Gilliland, and McNew rode in on fagged horses and appeared gravelly concerned about some matter. As it happened, though, the prosecution possessed a copy of Maxwell's earlier testimony and read it to the jurors.

Fall objected to the reading of Maxwell's testimony but was overruled. When it was his turn to question the witness, Maxwell replied that he had known Lee, Gilliland, and McNew for many years, that his ranch was not far from Lee's, and that he was at the Dog Canyon ranch on February 1, 1896, where he spent the night. Contradicting his original testimony, he said that when he arrived, Lee was already there.

Fall determined that it would be an easy thing to attack Maxwell's credibility, so he pointed out to the jurors that Garrett had paid Maxwell $2,000 to testify against Lee, an impressive sum of money for the day. Fall also pointed out another salient fact: Maxwell had written a letter to a friend of Lee's stating that he would say that the rancher was forty miles away when Fountain disappeared.

Fall got Maxwell to admit that, following his initial testimony, that prosecution attorney William Childers arranged for him to take a job in Colorado Springs, Colorado, and that he paid his fare to leave New Mexico. Fall also got Maxwell to admit that Childers told him that he "had better go away as the defendants or their friends would kill you."

Maxwell proved to be a poor witness for the prosecution. He folded under direct questioning, sweated profusely, and appeared on the verge of sickness. Fall had him confused. It was the consensus of all present that Maxwell did more damage to the prosecution than to the defense.

It seemed apparent that someone had gotten to Maxwell and visited with him about what his testimony was to be. The Fountain disappearance and apparent murder was an important and significant event, and Maxwell was privy to vital information. It is absurd to think that he would have forgotten his earlier testimony, and his behavior on the witness stand and his reaction to Fall's questioning was evidence that he was nervous and frightened. The only person he could possibly have been nervous and frightened about was Oliver Lee. It is likely that Maxwell was in fear for his life.

The next witness was Dr. Francis Crosson. Crosson explained that he had examined an amount of blood-soaked earth near the Fountain wagon and concluded that it came from a human being. Crosson's scientific terms and language confused the interpreter as well as the jurors.

When Fall asked Crosson if he could swear that the blood was from a human, the doctor backtracked, stating that he could not, that no one could tell human blood from any other kind. In spite of his statement, he went on to reiterate that his conclusion was that the blood he examined was that of a human being.

Seizing on Crosson's contradictory statements, Fall pounded away at him relentlessly. At one point he asked Crosson if he could tell whether "blood came from a horse, a coyote, a rabbit, or a man?" Crosson admitted he did not know. He then stated that "Blood testing is so difficult that the best expert in the world could not swear to it." Having accomplished what he set to do, Fall dismissed the intimidated witness.

Albert Fountain, Jr. was called to the stand. Earlier he had claimed that on finding his father's white horse there appeared to be blood on one side. During his testimony, he said, "something wide had been thrown on the horse's back like a blanket, causing him to sweat on his side and be dyed by the blanket or whatever it was." Then, Fountain, Jr. admitted, "I did not find any blood on the horse."

Thus far, the witnesses for the prosecution were providing more ammunition for the defense than the prosecution was comfortable with.

Riley Baker, Jim Gilliland's brother-in-law, testified that Gilliland told him that "the bodies would never be found and that no one would ever be convicted of murder. Fall pointed out to the jury that Baker did not get along with Gilliland and McNew and that he had reported to law officials on their doings and whereabouts in the past.

Next up was Frank Wayne whose ranch was located twenty-five miles from Lee's. On the day prior to Fountain's disappearance, Wayne and his brother were on Lee's ranch looking for a stray pony. During his search, Wayne encountered Lee who warned told him to "say nothing about what you saw here, as it might interfere with some of our plans." Whatever Wayne saw was never made clear. Fall declined to cross-examine.

The next witness for the prosecution was Pat Garrett. It was expected that Garrett would wrap up the case for the prosecution. He spoke of his background and his efforts to investigate the Fountain disappearance. During the trial. Garrett and Fall went back and forth with neither getting the upper hand. It the end, however, it was determined that Garrett contributed little that was helpful to the prosecution. After Garrett was dismissed, it was time for Albert Fall to present the defense.

Unlike the prosecution, Fall had selected his witnesses carefully, all individuals who could and would state authoritatively as to the whereabouts of Oliver Lee *et al* during the disappearance of Colonel Fountain. Sheriff George Curry of Otero County, an unabashed Lee and Fall sympathizer, stated that Jack Maxwell had told him that Lee, Gilliland, and McNew had indeed been at the Lee ranch at the time Fountain vanished. Bud Smith echoed Curry's remarks. Albert Blevins, a railroad employee, testified that he was at the Lee ranch during the time of the disappearance and that all three men were there. Oliver Lee's mother was called to the stand where she testified that her son had been home the day of the disappearance.

Then, Oliver Lee was called to the witness stand. Lee stated that he had never left his ranch during the time in question, and therefore was not aware that Fountain and his son were missing. He learned of the matter several days later, he claimed. He also said that once he learned he was a suspect in the case, he went immediately to Las Cruces to surrender, but that because he heard that there was talk of mob action and violence he changed his mind and, for his own safety, returned to his ranch.

Lee's brother-in-law Print Rhode testified that Major Llewellyn had threatened to blow up Lee's ranch house. Whether true or not, this statement had the effect on the jurors of placing the prosecution in a bad light. When Catron and his team vigorously denied this, it was clear that the jurors did not believe them.

One of Lee's ranch hands, a man named A. N. Bailey (no relation to Todd Bailey), was called to the stand. Bailey proved to be effective and believable. He told the jury that he had worked alongside Oliver Lee for the entire afternoon of February 1, 1896, and that there was no way that he could have ridden the fifty miles to Chalk Hill.

After the testimony of a few more witnesses, the defense rested. And it was time for final arguments. Following a short break, Todd Bailey and the other two Lee ranch cowhands resumed their previous positions in the courtroom. Bailey was now wearing his saddle slicker, and hidden underneath its folds was a shotgun. Earlier in the day, Bailey had shortened both the barrel and the stock. Lee's other two cowhands were similarly armed.

Years later, Todd Bailey stated that if Lee had been found guilty, he and the other two cowhands were to rise up and shoot Garrett, the other deputies, and the prosecuting attorneys. Following this, according to a previously arranged plan, they were to spirit Lee out of the building and ride to a location outside of town where more Lee ranch hands were waiting. From there, the plan was to travel several miles on horseback with a pair of hands splitting off from time to time to confuse trackers. Lee and Bailey would then continue on to Mexico.

In a move that solidified the notion that the prosecution team had no clue as to how to deal appropriately with the jury, they selected Richmond P. Barnes to open the final arguments. Barnes fancied himself a skilled orator and approached the task as a thespian would embrace a theatrical role. He rattled on, often quoting from Charles Dickens' *The Pickwick Papers*. The jurors knew nothing of Dickens and Barnes accomplished little but confusing them, assuming they could understand anything Barnes was saying at all. Even the interpreter seemed confused. The final arguments for the prosecution were off to a bad start.

After Barnes finally sat down, William B. Childers took over, though it was unclear how he could repair the damage recently just inflicted by his colleague. Childers argued that Lee remained on the run from the law for three years because he knew he was guilty of the charges. He claimed that the argument that they were afraid Garrett wanted to kill them was unsound. He pointed out that McNew had been in Garrett's custody for months and had gone unmolested. He further argued that Garrett's payment of $2,000 to Maxwell for his testimony against Lee was within the ethical bounds of the law. None of this impressed the jurors; quite the opposite.

Like Barnes, Childers rambled on and on. By the time he sat down, Fall noticed that many of the jurors were on the verge of falling asleep. He decided to use their fatigue to his advantage. Fall rose and walked over to the jury box. He praised them for their diligence and likewise lauded the legal system and the manner in which it served those who found themselves in difficulty. He pointed out that Jack Maxwell was a proven liar, and that his previous testimony art the first trial had been contradicted by no less than eight witnesses. Appealing to the sentiments of the jurors, Fall described Doña Ana County officials as "a lot of broken down political hacks...gathered together, as does the slimy filth on the edges of a dead eddy." As opposed to being bored to tears and put to sleep by Barnes and Childers, the jurors were now rising to the occasion, now interested in where this argument might be going.

Fall used this opportunity to point out to the jurors, for the most part poor residents of Hillsboro, that the territory spent a great deal of money, money from their taxes, to prosecute Lee and his companions. He looked the jurors in their eyes and informed them that the defendants, whom he described as "salt-of-the-earth working men" like themselves, were forced to pay for their defense out of their own pockets.

Fall was just getting warmed up. He related that the defendants were charged with the killing of Henry Fountain, but that no body had ever been found. He then said that, based on the evidence presented by the prosecution, "you would not hang a yellow dog." Fall turned away from the jurors and strode toward his seat as the entire courtroom, save for members of the prosecution team, burst into applause that lasted several minutes.

Amid this scene and the outflow of enthusiasm and energy directed toward Fall, and thus the defendants, Thomas Catron rose for rebuttal. It was already late in the evening, and much to the dismay of the jurors, as well as everyone else in the courtroom, Catron spoke for another two-and-a-half hours. It is doubtful that many were listening; jurors and spectators alike were falling asleep. It was clear the jury was desperate to be excused.

Catron's plan to orate for so long was not a brilliant move, but Fall's next move was. By the time Catron was ready to sit down, Fall was aware that the jurors had strong negative feelings about the prosecution, and he did not want them to get over them. It was eleven-thirty in the evening. Fall moved that the jury adjourn and render a verdict before retiring for the night. Todd Bailey and his companions checked their weapons and readied themselves for the final decision.

When the jury was called back in and seated, Lee and Gilliland, accompanied by Fall, were ordered to stand to receive the verdict. With little in the way of preliminaries, it was announced: Not guilty.

The courthouse erupted with applause, cheering, shouting, and laughter. The celebration lasted for more than an hour.

Catron and company closed their briefcases and slunk away. Having seen what they were up against in a courtroom with Albert Fall, they later elected not to activate the charges against Lee and Gilliland for the murders of Colonel Fountain and Kearney.

The decision was a blow to Garrett, both personally and professionally. He had spent three years bringing Fountain's killers into a courtroom only to have them set free. His investigation had yielded little that was useful, and what scant evidence that had been gathered was fumbled by the inept prosecution team.

On the other side of the courtroom, Oliver Lee was all smiles and accepting the handshakes, backslaps, and congratulations from well wishers. Standing nearby was Todd Bailey.

It was not over. Lee would tangle with Garrett again, and the next time only one would emerge alive. It was also not the last time Todd Bailey would be assigned a role relative to Sheriff Garrett.

[illegible] in the [illegible] of the coronation. Oliver Lee was all smiles and accepting [illegible] handshakes and congratulations [illegible] well-wishers. Standing nearby was [illegible].

[illegible] we [illegible] would mingle with [illegible] again, and the next one [illegible] would emerge [illegible] not [illegible] should be assigned a role [illegible] to [illegible].

27
MORE GUNPLAY

Following several years of agitation, excitement, and tension, all culminating in the not guilty verdict in the trial for the killing of Henry Fountain, things began to settle down for Oliver Lee. No longer were there warrants for his arrest; Lee was now a free man, and he was relieved to not have to deal with Pat Garrett any longer. Little did Lee know that Garrett would eventually find his way back into the rancher's affairs.

Talk of the Fountain killings continued, despite the not-guilty verdict, and every cowman and town resident had a theory about what happened as well as the identity of the killers. The names Oliver Lee, Bill McNew, and Jim Gilliland were on the lips of many, but few dared to mention them out loud. Even noted train robber Thomas "Black Jack" Ketchum was suspected of being involved in the killings. His brother, Sam, told Magdalena lawman Bob Lewis that Black Jack murdered Fountain and his little boy, and that he, Sam, was an eyewitness to the killing. Evidence for Ketchum's involvement, however, is non-existent.

Oliver Lee continued to frequent Alamogordo, Las Cruces, and El Paso for a variety of reasons, many of them associated with his ranching enterprises. When he stepped into a hotel or tavern, all conversation stopped and he was the recipient of furtive glances. In spite of the suspicions, however, Lee could still claim a number of close friends and allies, most of them fellow cowmen, as well as others who were convinced that New Mexico was better off with Albert Jennings Fountain out of the picture.

Though a free man, Oliver Lee remained cautious. Whenever he embarked on a trip, he departed before daylight and never told anyone where he was going. He never sat in a lighted room in the evening with the shades up. It was reported that Lee was a light sleeper, and that he always kept a horse saddled in his barn in the event he needed to make a quick escape. A story was told that Lee had a tunnel constructed, one that ran from his Dog Canyon house to an outbuilding several dozen yards away. Some claimed to have seen the tunnel, and today the interpretive guide at the Oliver Lee State Park speaks of the existence of the tunnel as fact.

In 1907, Lee was once again in the news, this time as a result of a conflict over water rights. An Otero County newspaper publisher named J. C. Smith, along with four other men, filed a claim on the water emanating from Dog Canyon, the same water that Frenchy availed himself of and used to irrigate his orchard and garden, and the same water than ran down the canyon and onto Oliver Lee's ranch. Smith and company had held the claim for two years, it was claimed, before it reverted to Lee.

In March 1907, Lee was involved in a confrontation over a fence. One of Lee's nieces held a claim near the rancher's Dog Canyon headquarters. The boundary between her claim and the neighbor's was unclear. One morning, the niece spotted James R. Fennimore, his father-in-law Tom Knight, and two Fennimore ranch hands erecting a fence in the disputed area. The niece informed Lee, who was on the scene a short time later. A disagreement ensued, and the result was a gun fight with rifles and revolvers. By the time it was over, Fennimore had been shot in the hip by Lee.

Lee rode into Alamogordo to report the incident, and had warrants made out for Fennimore, Knight, and the two ranch hands. Fennimore likewise made it into Alamogordo where he provided his version of the event, claiming that Lee had tried to kill him, and likewise had warrants made out against him. Lee explained that if he had wanted to kill Fennimore he would have shot him in the head. Nothing ever came of the confrontation and the case was dismissed.

Lee's ranch continued to prosper, and his cattle and horses brought top dollar during sale time. It was said that by now, Oliver Lee was related to half the people in the Tularosa Basin, and that his relatives, friends, in-laws, and neighbors stood by him through thick and thin. He had a house constructed in Alamogordo that became a gathering place for many in the area. The gracious Mrs. Winnie Lee served fine dinners and the door was always open for friends.

28
ENTER WAYNE BRAZEL

While events and the momentum of his earlier, troublesome days had slowed down somewhat for Oliver Lee, the life of his adversary, Pat Garrett, continued to spiral into complications, problems, and trials. Each day was worse than the previous. Garrett owed money to prominent people and institutions throughout southern New Mexico and clear up to the capitol in Santa Fe. He was not an easy man to get along with under the best of circumstances, and his abrasive personality, one often fueled with alcohol, did not help matters.

Garrett's list of enemies was growing longer. He had gone from being mildly disliked by many in Doña Ana County to being completely despised. When he came to town, he insulted and threatened people, sought quarrels, and occasionally picked fights in the streets.

Added to Garrett's list of enemies was rancher W. W. Cox, a close friend of and in-law to Oliver Lee. William Webb Cox was born in DeWitt County, Texas on November 2, 1854. When he was nineteen years old, his father was killed during the Sutton-Taylor Feud. A short time later, Cox left Texas, bound for New Mexico. In explaining the reasons for his departure, an account has him killing a man, a physician. Learning that there was a warrant for his arrest, he fled DeWitt County, never to return. Cox acquired his ranch in 1893, became a successful and respected cattleman, and eventually expanded his holdings to over 150,000 acres.

Earlier, Garrett borrowed money from Cox whose ranch was nearby, and put his cattle herd up as equity. Cox loaned him $3,567. Until such time as the debt was paid off, Cox moved the herd over to his own ranch. Like most people in New Mexico by this time, Cox did not trust Garrett. Garrett in turn was annoyed by the fact that Cox maintained control of his cattle herd and informed him he would continue to do so until the mortgage on his ranch was paid off. Garrett explained to Cox that without the cattle he was unable to make any money, but Cox remained steadfast. Garrett's hatred for Cox grew by the day. Garrett moved his family to Las Cruces in hopes that opportunities there would be greater.

President Theodore Roosevelt appointed George Curry to serve as governor of New Mexico, and Garrett was certain that Curry, in turn, would appoint him to the position of superintendent of the new territorial prison at Santa Fe. Why Garrett believed such an appointment would be forthcoming is unclear, and Curry never made such an offer. Desperate for money, Garrett moved again, this time to El Paso where he took a job selling real estate. He left his family in Las Cruces.

While in El Paso, Garrett took up with a prostitute, a woman known only as Mrs. Brown. The two were often seen dining and drinking together and riding through town in a buggy. It is not known how much real estate Garrett managed to sell in El Paso, but it was clear he was spending a lot of money on liquor. While Garrett was away from the ranch, his son Poe had taken over as manager. In Garrett's absence, Poe made an arrangement with a Doña Ana cowboy named Jesse Wayne Brazel to lease the Bear Canyon portion of the ranch for five years. Papers were signed on March 11, 1907. Brazel was to figure prominently in the life of Pat Garrett for the next eleven-and-a-half months.

Brazel was born in Kansas in 1876. Shortly thereafter, the family moved to Lincoln County, New Mexico, and then on to a location known as Gold Camp that bordered the Cox ranch and was not far from the Garrett ranch. Brazel found employment on the Cox ranch; he was regarded as hardworking, dependable, and uncomplaining. Brazel did not drink and was adept at breaking horses, and W. W. Cox was impressed by the youth's competence and loyalty. In many ways, Cox served as a mentor to the young man, and many thought the two were related. In turn, Brazel saw Cox as a role model and inspiration. Brazel courted Olive Elizabeth Boyd who was living in the home of Print Rhode, Cox's brother-in-law. The two eventually married.

In addition to working as a cowhand on the Cox Ranch, Brazel cast about for other ways to make more money. He and Rhode decided one way to do that was to raise goats. Goats required little maintenance and grazed on the same forage as cattle. They also turned a high profit. Many cattle ranchers cared little for goats because, they claimed, the animals ruined pastures for cattle grazing. Pat Garrett, in particular, hated goats. Brazel and Rhode deemed that the Bear Canyon area of Garrett's ranch was entirely suitable for the goat herd. Knowing Garrett was out of town, Brazel approached Poe about leasing the acreage. During the discussion, Brazel did not mention Rhode's name, nor did he mention that goats were involved. The terms of the lease called for Brazel to pay Poe ten heifer calves and one filly colt, leaving the impression that that was the kind of livestock to be placed on the land

As soon as he learned of the arrangement, and became aware of Rhode's involvement, the elder Garrett flew into an extended cursing rage. He not only despised goats, he also hated Print Rhode, a deep animosity that stemmed from an earlier incident at the Cox Ranch.

The event that turned Rhode against Garrett forever involved a hunt for a wanted murderer from Oklahoma who had found employment at the Cox Ranch, a man named Norman Newman, alias Billy Reed. Garrett and Deputy José Espalin arrived at the ranch and, revolvers in hand, made their way on foot to a position behind the house. After crossing the back yard and stepping up to the kitchen door, Garrett spotted a man washing dishes. Garrett asked the man if he was Reed. When the man replied that he was, Garrett told him he was under arrest.

As Garrett stepped forward, he unaccountably holstered his revolver. One second later, Reed slammed a punch into the sheriff's face. Garrett pulled handcuffs from his belt, swung them, and cracked Reed across the head and knocking him to the floor. As the two lawmen fell atop Reed and tried to cuff him, they were attacked by a large bulldog that had charged into the kitchen from an adjacent room. The bulldog belonged to Albert Fall. Fall was serving as Cox's lawyer and left the animal temporarily in the care of his client. During the melee, Reed broke free and ran toward the smokehouse where he knew Cox kept a revolver. As Reed entered the doorway of the smokehouse, he was struck by two bullets in the back. He was killed instantly. Garrett and Espalin loaded Reed's corpse into the buckboard and returned with him to Las Cruces.

Several days later when W. W. Cox returned home from a trip to Mexico, he learned of what transpired between Garrett and Norman Newman and became incensed. He was particularly concerned that his pregnant wife had been subjected to the violence and killing inflicted by Garrett and his deputy. Cox's anger, however, was nothing compared to the outrage expressed by Print Rhode. When Rhode learned what had happened and of the terror experienced by his sister, Rhode swore to any and all who would listen that he was going to kill Garrett.

Not only did Garrett already have a formidable enemy in Oliver Lee, he had angered W. W. Cox, one of southern New Mexico's biggest and most influential ranchers, even more than he already had. And now he managed to add the volatile and angry Print Rhode to the list. It was soon to grow longer.

Wayne Brazel

29
ILLEGAL CHINESE LABORERS

During the late 1800s and early 1900s, hundreds of miles of railroad were constructed throughout Mexico, most of the work undertaken by imported Chinese laborers. The Chinese arrived in Mexico with promises of steady work at decent pay. Though the work was constant—twelve hours per day, seven days per week—the pay was dismal, and the Chinese families lived in poverty.

By the time the Mexican Revolution was winding down, most of the railroads had been built and hundreds of Chinese now found themselves out of work. They set their sights north of the border and undertook a migration in that direction. At the time, however, the United States was not welcoming to Chinese immigrants and refused them access. In spite of the establishment of the 1882 Chinese Exclusion Act that placed a moratorium on Chinese labor, it has been estimated that at least 17,000 illegal Chinese immigrants entered the U. S. to fill vacant jobs over the next forty years. For some, brokering illegal Chinese laborers became a lucrative enterprise.

A significant percentage of the Chinese crossed illegally, and most were transported by contractors who were hired to provide laborers for railroad construction, mines, and farms in southern Colorado. Dozens, if not hundreds, had been crossed in this manner, and a staging area was sought where they could remain until the time arrived for them to move on to Colorado. The demand for labor in Colorado was great, with thousands of jobs waiting. The person, or agency, that could provide such help stood to make a great deal of money from smuggling and transporting available laborers, and the Chinese represented a commodity. The temptation to make significant money by smuggling illegal Chinese attracted a group of men in southern New Mexico. They included Oliver Lee, W. W. Cox, Print Rhode, Carl Adamson, Mannen Clements, and Jim Miller.

Mannen Clements was serving as a constable in El Paso, and from time to time came in contact with Oliver Lee. As constable, Clements busied himself with shaking down prostitutes and bullying most whom he came in contact with. Clements was an unsavory character. A cousin of outlaw John Wesley Hardin and the brother-in-law of "Killin' Jim" Miller, Clements was a known cattle rustler and killer of men. He also found employment as a sometime gun for hire.

Texan Jim Miller led a varied life holding down jobs as a ranch hand, a deputy sheriff, and a Texas Ranger. As a lawman, Miller was known to have penchant for killing Mexicans. Despite his illegal and unsavory activities, Miller was a devout Christian and an avid churchgoer, and was never known to drink or curse. After moving to Fort Worth, Texas, in 1900, Miller advertised himself as a professional assassin. He charged $150 for each killing. It is estimated that Miller assassinated well over a dozen individuals prior to allegedly being invited to El Paso by Mannen Clements. His weapon of choice was a shotgun.

Information related to the smuggling operation came to light from Dr. W. C. Field, a Las Cruces physician. One day, Field was called to treat a man for some undisclosed ailment. On arriving, Field saw that his patient was Chinese, a man who had been smuggled across the border at El Paso and was currently residing in the county jail at Las Cruces. As he was being treated, the Chinaman revealed to Dr. Field the smuggling arrangements and named many who were involved. On returning to his office, Field wrote a letter containing this information to U. S. Marshal Creighton Foraker, who in turn passed it on to other federal agents. Following this, U. S. Marshal and Secret Service Agent Fred Fornoff was assigned to look into the matter. Much of what follows is derived from Fornoff's investigation reports.

As numbers of Chinese were smuggled across the Mexican border at El Paso and some New Mexico locations, the smugglers were in need of a remote and safe place to hold the immigrants until such time as they could transport them north into Colorado. Lee and Cox determined that Garrett's Bear Canyon Ranch was considered ideal for this purpose. In order for this plan to work, however, it was necessary to get Brazel's goats off of the ranch. Lee, Cox, and others decided on a plan. Enlisting Carl Adamson and Jim Miller, it was agreed that the two men would approach Garrett about leasing his Bear Canyon Ranch to hold a herd of over one thousand head of cattle they claimed they intended to bring up from Mexico. They offered Garrett top dollar for the use of his ranch to fatten the cattle up until such time as they could move the herd to Oklahoma. The truth was that Adamson and Miller had no cattle. They wanted the place to hide the Chinese. The only hitch in the plan was that Wayne Brazel held a lease for said acreage on which he had placed his herd of goats.

Garrett, on seeing a chance for some easy money, was attracted to the proposition presented by Adamson and Miller. He told them that he was willing to deal with them, but that the property was currently under lease to a goat herder. Garrett explained that if the lease could be broken and the goats moved elsewhere, then he would agree to the deal advanced by Adamson and Miller.

Brazel was at first unwilling to cancel the lease, but then agreed to move out if he were paid $3.50 per head. He said he had twelve hundred goats. Miller agreed to the deal and had a contract executed. Meeting with Garrett later in Las Cruces, Miller offered him $3,000 for the Bear Canyon property. Miller also told Garrett that if he would agree to the deal, he would hire him to drive the cattle from Mexico to the ranch. Garrett was overjoyed with his newfound luck and the prospect of some significant money coming in. Excited, he resigned from his real estate job, picked up his family in Las Cruces, and moved back to the ranch. He was unprepared for the difficulties that would follow.

After Garrett returned to his ranch, Brazel sent word to him that he had misquoted the number of goats on the property. Instead of the twelve hundred goats he originally mentioned, he informed Garrett that there were eighteen hundred. In his message, Brazel also stated that unless he was paid for every one of the goats he would not agree to withdraw from the lease. When Miller was informed of these conditions, he told Garrett that the agreement would be cancelled.

Given these new developments, Garrett feared he would not receive the money he had anticipated. In addition, the plans of Oliver Lee and the others for a remote and secure location to house the smuggled Chinese laborers were thwarted. It was clear to Lee *et al* that Garrett would eventually figure out that no cattle were forthcoming. It is believed that, knowing well that Garrett was deep in debt, they considered offering the ex-lawman a piece of the action. The main problem with this strategy was that Lee and Garrett were sworn enemies and hated one another. In addition, Garrett was very uncomfortable around W. W. Cox and Print Rhode, and was perhaps in fear of both men. It soon became clear to Lee that if Garrett were invited to come in on the smuggling plot, he would not only refuse but was likely to alert law enforcement officials. In this manner, Garrett was in the position of exacting a certain amount of revenge against men who had tormented him in the past, some of whom he owned a lot of money.

To Oliver Lee, there was only one clear solution to the problem: Pat Garrett had to go.

30
RAILROAD TIES

While Oliver Lee was pondering what to do with Pat Garrett, a unique business opportunity presented itself, one that had the potential to make a great deal of money to men savvy enough to make the enterprise work.

For years, there was talk of running a railroad line from El Paso, Texas, to Alamogordo, New Mexico, and eventually all the way up to Chicago. The first official attempt came in 1895 with the El Paso, St. Louis, and Chicago Railway and Telegraph Company undertaking the planning and construction. It was known as the El Paso and Northeastern Railway. When the line to Alamogordo was completed, little time was lost in the building of a branch line stretching from Alamogordo the pine and fir forests of the Sacramento Mountains to the east. The rationale for this new line, called the Alamogordo and Sacramento Mountain Railway, extended into Cloudcroft in 1900. Its main purpose was to haul logs harvested from the forests and transport them back down to an Alamogordo sawmill. There, they were converted them into railroad ties that were necessary for the continued construction of the railway northward.

Recognizing a grand opportunity, a cabal of confederates organized a company to supply railroad ties to the EP&NE Railway. It is unclear who came up with the idea, but the company consisted of Oliver Lee, Albert B. Fall, W. H. H. Llewelyn, Llewelyn's son Morton, George Curry, and W. A. Hawkins, a former law partner of Fall's and at the time an attorney for the EP&NE Railway.

After being cut, the logs were loaded onto A&SM Railway flatcars and hauled into Alamogordo where they were transferred to a sawmill and transformed into the railroad ties that were sold to the EP&NE Railway. While the timber harvesting company made impressive profits, the truth was that its activities were illegal.

For one thing, it is believed by many that most, if not all, of the timber cutting was accomplished with illegal Chinese laborers brought to the site be Oliver Lee and his partners. For another, the timbers were cut from federal land without permission, also illegal

When, after a period of time, it became clear that laws were being broken and the risk of penalties severe, the timber cutting and railroad tie company was dissolved. Lee, Fall, Curry, and Hawkins returned to their regular routines. The father and son Llewelyns were, at the time, both federal employees. As a result of their involvement in the illegal activities, they lost their jobs.

Somehow, Pat Garrett learned of the timber harvesting operation on government property, the manufacture and sale of railroad ties, and the employment of illegal Chinese laborers. It has been assumed by some that Garrett wanted to be cut in on the scheme, as he was desperately in need of money. It is more likely, however, that Garrett would have been uncomfortable, even intimidated, being in a shady business with Lee and his associates, all of whom despised him. Garrett, as it turned out, was in a unique position to undertake revenge on his enemies by reporting their activities to the authorities. This notion, along with other ongoing difficulties, provided Oliver Lee additional reason to get rid of Pat Garrett.

31
THE PLOT TO REMOVE GARRETT

According to U. S. secret agent Fred Fornoff, the mastermind behind the plot to get Garrett out of the way was Oliver Lee, with considerable input from his brother-in-law W. W. Cox, along with Print Rhode.

By this time Lee had developed a pattern to the way he handled certain "business" difficulties. His principal business was his successful and growing ranching empire, but Lee dabbled in other enterprising ventures, the illegal smuggling of Chinese laborers being one, the illegal harvesting of lumber for railroad ties from federal lands for another. When someone stepped forward in an attempt to interrupt or obstruct his money-making arrangements, Lee's *modus operandi* was to simply get rid of them.

As far as is known, the first official who undertook to gather evidence related to Oliver Lee's cattle rustling and brand-altering activities was Les Dow, the stock inspector hired by the New Mexico Stock Growers Association and who reported to and took orders from Colonel Fountain. Though significant time had passed and Lee escaped prosecution based on Dow's evidence, he knew the inspector still possessed damaging evidence. Lee said that the most efficient way to eliminate the problem was to eliminate the person involved. As a result, Les Dow was killed and now permanently out of the picture. Lee orchestrated Dow's murder, sending his trusted and loyal employee and nephew, Todd Bailey, to do the job.

Fountain, the dogged prosecutor for the cattle association who was only days away from having Lee arrested and charged with cattle rustling and brand-altering was out of the picture as a result of Lee's plotting. Lee knew he stood little chance in court given the evidence possessed by Fountain, evidence initially supplied by Les Dow. The simplest way to handle this problem was, in Lee's mind, was to get rid of Fountain.

The plan to kill Fountain was a slightly revised version of the one developed in 1894. The movements of Fountain were followed as he traveled from his home in Las Cruces to the courthouse in Lincoln. Lee, Gilliland, and McNew rode ahead of Fountain on his way back to Las Cruces to make certain of his route and to determine the timing of his travels. Waiting ahead at a selected location at Chalk Hill was the shooter, the reliable and dependable Todd Bailey. Fountain was dispatched with two shots. It was unfortunate that eight-year-old Henry Fountain was along on the trip with his father, but Lee was determined to leave no witnesses. It was part of the cost of doing business.

And now, Pat Garrett, long a thorn in the side of Oliver Lee, was standing in the way of the rancher's smuggling venture. Lee had had enough of Garrett and was bound to be rid of him once and for all. Now was the time.

The plot to eliminate Garrett was somewhat involved, and it included several participants. Investigator Fred Fornoff reported rumors he heard that rancher W. W. Cox was putting up an amount of money to have Pat Garrett killed. The contact man, according to Fornoff, was Mannen Clements, part time El Paso constable. Clements allegedly met with Cox in the El Paso law office of Albert B. Fall where he was handed fifteen hundred dollars. Clements, as the rumors had it, was to use the money to hire "Killin' Jim" Miller to pull the trigger and to pay Carl Adamson to act as a witness. Cox would then talk to Wayne Brazel and convince him to take the blame for the killing, assuring the cowhand that he would never be convicted.

The plot to kill Garrett expanded. Though rumors abounded, historians generally agree that a second meeting was held at El Paso's St. Regis Hotel. Attending were Oliver Lee, W. W. Cox, Albert B. Fall, Bill McNew, Jim Miller, Carl Adamson, Print Rhode, Mannen Clements, and Wayne Brazel. This meeting took place prior to the establishment of Brazel's goat herd on Garrett's Bear Canyon Ranch. Most are convinced that Cox called for the meeting. According to author Sonnichsen, Cox agreed to pay for the killing, but stated that it needed to appear as an act of self-defense.

Oliver Lee came up with a workable plan. In his vision of the removal of Garrett, Lee suggested that Wayne Brazel, a quiet, mild-mannered, and dependable ranch hand, lease Garrett's Bear Canyon Ranch from son Poe Garrett and place a herd of goats on it. Garrett hated goats, and when he learned of the transaction and confronted Brazel about it, as all knew he would, the ensuing disagreement would provide an excuse to kill him. It was agreed that any and all would be sympathetic to Brazel if he shot in "self defense," and that it was unlikely that any jury would convict him. It was acknowledged that Brazel was unskilled and inexperienced in the use of firearms, and that he rarely carried a revolver. Garrett, on the other hand, was known to be belligerent, short-tempered, and prone to pick fights. It was suggested that someone else would have to perform the actual killing.

The question was: Who was to be the shooter, the man to take down the once-famous lawman, Pat Garrett? Jim Miller was mentioned, but he was a high-profile assassin and would be suspected. Oliver Lee had the answer. In his employ was a man who had the skill, a man who owed everything to Lee, and would do anything for his employer. A man who had killed before at Lee's request and would do it again this time. Oliver Lee argued in favor of Todd Bailey, and it was agreed he would pull the trigger. Jim Miller was to be his backup.

It was determined that it would be necessary to get Garrett out of his home and away from his ranch. To accomplish this, Carl Adamson was to pick him up in a buckboard and carry him toward Las Cruces where Garrett believed he was to meet with Wayne Brazel. If Garrett could be convinced that the meeting was called to facilitate the agreement to lease the Bear Canyon Ranch to Miller, and that a sizeable amount of money would change hands, it was presumed the desperate ex-lawman would jump at the opportunity.

On the way to Las Cruces, Garrett was to be ambushed. At a designated location, Adamson would stop the buckboard using the excuse that he had to urinate. Prior to halting the vehicle, Wayne Brazil, who would have positioned himself along the road, would ride up and engage Garrett in conversation. Once the vehicle was stopped, Adamson was to climb down and Brazel was to back away, leaving Garrett isolated. From a vantage point, the shooter, using a rifle, would kill Garrett. Brazel would take the blame, confess to the killing, and plead self defense. Carl Adamson would serve as a witness.

The plotters went over the scheme several times and discerned no flaws in it. Knowing that Garrett was deep in debt and with the prospect of coming into a significant amount of money, they were certain that he would readily take the bait. They were correct.

32
THE ASSASSINATION OF PAT GARRETT

The momentum related to eliminating Pat Garrett took a significant step forward on the afternoon of February 28, 1908. One of the planners, Carl Adamson, drove a two-horse buggy up to the Garrett ranch where he was greeted by the former lawman and his wife, Apolinaria. Adamson was there to pick up Garrett and transport him to Las Cruces where the two were scheduled to meet with Wayne Brazel in an attempt, Garrett believed, to settle the problem with the goatherd.

Mrs. Garrett had a bad feeling about Adamson the moment he entered the house. She confessed her concerns and suspicions to her husband who found them amusing. Garrett told his wife that Adamson was the key to future financial independence. Adamson was invited to spend the night in the Garrett home.

The following morning after breakfast, Garrett and Adamson prepared to set out for Las Cruces. Garrett's horse was tied to the back of the buggy for the return trip. After telling his family goodbye, Garrett climbed into the seat next to Adamson and drove away. It was the last time any of his family saw him alive.

The road followed by Adamson passed the tiny community of Gold Camp, into and across San Augustín Pass, and through the small village of Organ. A short distance out of Organ, Adamson pulled up at Russell Walter's livery stable. As Adamson guided the horses toward a water trough, Garrett visited with Willis Walter, the son of the proprietor. According to an interview with Walter in 1968, Garrett asked him if he had seen Wayne Brazel. The question seems an odd one, since Garrett and Adamson were expecting to meet Brazel in Las Cruces. Walter told Garrett that Brazel had been there, but rode away a few minutes prior to Adamson pulling in. Walter said he traveled in the direction Adamson was taking. The odd presence of Brazel at Watson's livery instead of waiting for him at Las Cruces should have alerted Garrett to the notion something was afoot. If it did, he gave no indication of such.

South of Organ the road forked, the two routes extending for two miles before rejoining. One of the roads was known as Mail-Scott Road, the other called Freighter's Road. Freighter's Road was more suitable for handling the traffic from the heavy ore wagons that traversed it. It was shorter but considerably rougher, thus most travelers preferred the Mail-Scott Road. As Adamson neared the junction, Garrett spotted Brazel some distance down the Mail-Scott Road in conversation with an unidentified man on horseback. A moment later, the stranger rode away.

Historians, along with a number of enthusiasts, suggest the unidentified man was Print Rhode. This, at best, is a poor guess. If Adamson and Garrett were able to identify Brazel at that distance, then Rhode, who was well known to both men, would have been easily recognized. Accumulating evidence points strongly to the notion that the rider was Todd Bailey, Oliver Lee's ranch hand and nephew. If true, it is therefore probable that Brazel alerted Bailey to the fact that Garrett and Adamson were on the way, giving Bailey time to get set up.

Minutes later, Adamson and Garrett caught up with Brazel. Adamson did not halt the buggy for conversation but continued traveling down the Mail-Scott Road toward Las Cruces. Brazel fell in behind them, following closely. Garrett and Brazel did not like each other, and the two men did little more than acknowledge the presence of each other with a nod. According to articles in the *El Paso Herald* and the *Rio Grande Republican*, Brazel sometimes rode ahead of the buggy and at other times behind it. When the road was wide enough, he traveled alongside the buggy. At one point during the trip, Adamson asked Brazel if his goats were kidding.

Finally, Garrett asked Brazel why he originally stated that he had twelve hundred goats and later changed the number to eighteen hundred. Brazel replied that he miscounted. The difference between twelve hundred and eighteen hundred should generate suspicion from any competent researcher, but this dramatic disparity has never been adequately addressed by historians during the more than a century that has elapsed since the event. The fact that the goat herd was claimed to be one-third larger than it was only weeks earlier should not be disregarded. The actual number of goats placed on the Bear Canyon range would surely have been known by Brazel, Rhode, and Miller. Even allowing time for kidding, it remains unlikely that the herd could have grown to such a size in that short amount of time. The questions must be asked: Were these numbers cooked up in order to delay or obviate Garrett's opportunity to place Adamson's cattle on the range? Was Garrett being set up the entire time?

Following a brief exchange between Garrett and Brazel, Adamson guided the buggy along a portion of the road that passed between a low ridge on his left and Alameda Arroyo on his right. At this point he pulled to a halt, claiming he needed to urinate. He handed the lines to Garrett, climbed down, and then walked to a position in front of the horses. The conversation between Garrett and Brazel had progressed to an argument when Brazel told him that he was not going to relinquish the lease. Garrett replied that he would get Brazel off the land one way or another.

At this point, according to Adamson, Garrett picked up the shotgun he had brought with him and climbed out of the buggy. Walking to the rear of the vehicle, with the shotgun in his right hand, he turned away from Brazel, removed the glove from his left hand, and had just begun to urinate. A second later, a bullet tore through his cranium. Garrett spun and fell to the ground, his head toward the ridge and his feet toward the arroyo. A moment later, a second bullet tore through his abdomen at a low angle and lodged in his upper body near a shoulder.

Pat Garrett, who made the mistake of getting on the wrong side of Oliver Lee, was dead.

33
THE MECHANICS OF THE ASSASSINATION

For well over a century the assassination of Pat Garrett has been discussed, analyzed, written about, and argued. And during all this time no one has gotten any closer to determining the identity of the man who pulled the trigger on the lawman. The suspects that have been advanced have included Wayne Brazel, "Killin' Jim" Miller, Print Rhode, Carl Adamson, and W. W. Cox. Each of these suspects has been eliminated for a variety of reasons. (see *Pat Garrett: The Man Behind the Badge,* Jameson)

Garrett's assassin was a man known to history, his name and role in a number of Oliver Lee-related enterprises and family connections appearing in literature over the years, his identity residing in the nooks and crannies of published history. For reasons not completely understood, he has been all but completely overlooked by historians. His name was Todd Bailey. (see "Background" on page 187.)

Acting on instructions from Oliver Lee, Todd Bailey rode ahead of Adamson's buggy out to a preselected location along the Mail-Scott Road. Along the way, he encountered Print Rhode and had a brief conversation with him before continuing. It was Bailey and Rhode that Garrett had seen on arriving at the junction of Mail Scott and Freighters Roads. Bailey hurried down the road and arrived at the eastern spur of the low ridge that paralleled the artery. He spurred his horse up the shallow slope to the crest of the ridge and rode to a point near its western edge. Here, Bailey, sitting atop his horse, looked down the north-facing slope and spotted the location selected earlier for the assassination, a point where the road crossed another. From his position on the ridge, Bailey could observe the road from Organ and easily pick out travelers. A few moments later, he spotted the buggy transporting Pat Garrett and Carl Adamson.

As the buggy drew closer to the crossroads near the bottom of the ridge, Bailey guided his horse down the south slope and out of sight of the road. On reaching the base of the slope, he tied his horse off to a mesquite tree. From a leather scabbard, he withdrew a .30 -.40 Krag, a lightweight lever-action carbine with a twenty-inch barrel, the weapon manufactured by Winchester, and one employed by the U. S. Army since 1892. Loaded and ready for shooting was a .30 -.40 smokeless powder cartridge popular with hunters.

On foot, Bailey rounded the western edge of the ridge, across the flat, sand and gravel desert dotted with creosote bush toward the road, crossed it, and proceeded another 130 feet to Alameda Arroyo. He positioned himself in what he perceived to be an ideal location in the shallow arroyo wherein he had a perfect field of fire at anything or anyone stopped near the crossroads. While he waited for the buggy to arrive, Bailey lit a hand-rolled cigarette and sat down on the bank to await his target.

Not much time passed before Bailey heard the jingle of traces and the clop of horse hooves approaching along the road. He rose from his position and spotted the buggy a short distance away. Adamson was holding the reins, Garrett the passenger, and Wayne Brazel was on horseback and maintaining a position to the left of the vehicle toward the rear. Bailey could hear Garrett and Brazel arguing.

At the pre-designated point, Adamson reined the horses to a halt and stated that he needed to urinate. After climbing down, Adamson walked to a spot in front of the animals. This placed him in a position such that he could grab the lines and keep the animals from bolting when the planned-for shot was fired. Brazel remained in his position on the rear near the left side of the buggy.

Garrett picked up his shotgun, climbed out of the buggy, walked behind it, and took a couple of steps to the right of the vehicle. While still arguing with Brazel, he pulled the glove from his left hand, unbuttoned his trousers, and began urinating. From his position near the bank of the arroyo, Todd Bailey had a clear line of fire. Brazel was positioned a sufficient distance to the left, and Adamson was far to the right near the horses. Garrett was between them, his back to Bailey. Bailey took aim and fired. The bullet entered the back of Garrett's head, close to the left ear, tore through his brain, and exited at the right eyebrow. Garrett was spun around, flailing his arms as he did so, and dropped to the ground on his back, his feet facing Bailey. Years later, Bailey stated that when Garrett hit the ground, the sound was "like you had dropped a sack of potatoes."

Bailey ejected the shell and inserted another, took aim at the prone Garrett, and fired a second shot. The bullet entered Garrett's lower stomach, proceeded at a low angle through the torso, and came to lodge near the left shoulder. Pat Garrett, once a famous lawman that had descended to the depths of shame and ridicule and had the misfortune of making an enemy of Oliver Lee was no more. (For an extensive and detailed account of the killing and the events leading up to it event, see *The Assassination of Pat Garrett,* W.C. Jameson, Two Dot Publishers, 2020.)

34
THE KILLING OF MANNEN CLEMENTS

With the killing of Pat Garrett, most of the loose ends that had potential to threaten the safety and livelihood of Oliver Lee appeared to have been tied up. Another, however, was soon to rise to the surface in the form of Mannen Clements, Jr.

Emmanuel "Mannen" Clements, Jr. had a past that involved cattle rustling and murder. The somewhat diminutive Clements—well under five-and-a-half feet tall—has been described as a rancher, a feudist, and a gunfighter. Clements occasionally hired out as an assassin, a profession he shared with his brother-in-law, "Killin' Jim" Miller. Some accounts state he was the father-in-law. At various times Clements served as a deputy constable, constable, and deputy sheriff, mostly for the city of El Paso, Texas. Clements relocated in El Paso in 1894 after killing a man in Alpine, Texas.

Clements learned that brother-in-law Miller was in jail in Oklahoma for the assassination of a rancher named Bobbitt. Clements went to A. B. Fall to solicit his help in getting Miller out of jail, but Fall informed Clements that his hands were tied, that he had little to no influence in Oklahoma. Clements implied to Fall that he would go to the authorities and reveal the plot to kill Garrett and name all that were involved in it, Fall included, if there was no help to free Miller forthcoming.

Fall lost no time in alerting Oliver Lee of Clements' threat to expose the Garrett plot. Lee reacted in his normal manner: The solution to the problem was to get rid of the witness. He began formulating plans to eliminate Mannen Clements, Jr.

Historians cannot agree on when Mannen Clements, Jr. was killed or by whom. The truth is that among the heretofore published materials on Clements, the "experts" engaged in little to no competent research and merely repeated what others had stated, or copied unsubstantiated materials. Clements' murderer has never been agreed upon, and until now had never been accurately identified.

One version of the story has Clements meeting his end in Ballinger, Texas, on March 29, 1887. Clements was close to intoxicated when a man identified as Joe Townsend approached him. The two men got into an argument, allegedly over recent election results. Both men drew and fired their weapons and Clements received a fatal wound. The truth: It was Emmanuel Clements, Sr., Mannen's father, who was shot down by Joe Townsend. Both father and son had the same names and as a result confused the historians, in spite of the fact that there was a twenty-one year span of time between the deaths of the two men. During their lifetimes, Clements, Sr. was called "Big Mannen," and Junior was called "Little Mannen."

Another version: Clements was drinking in the Coney Island Saloon in El Paso on December 29, 1908, when he was shot in the back of the head and killed by a man who was later identified as Joe Brown, a former El Paso constable. Brown, however, was never charged with the murder of Clements.

A third version, one that has come to light in the past few years, and one that carries considerably greater probability and veracity than the previous, has Clements' assassination planned and choreographed by Oliver Lee.

Over the years Lee and Fall had grown extremely close. Fall had served as Lee's lawyer on several occasions, and the two men had partnered in a number of business and political dealings. When Mannen Clements attempted to blackmail Fall with regard to the Garrett assassination, it was clear to the attorney that something needed to be done. Fall informed Lee of Clements' threat, and the two men determined they had much to lose should Clements' decide to make the plot public. Mannen Clements posed a threat to the safety and sanctity of the Lee-Fall empire, and he needed to be removed. Lee decided to take care of the situation, and he summoned Todd Bailey.

Bailey traveled to El Paso by train and checked into a hotel. He knew, or was made aware, of Clements' habit of drinking in the Coney Island

Saloon in the evenings. Around sundown on the evening of December 29, 1908, Clements was standing at his accustomed place at the bar. According to the few witnesses present, a well-dressed man walked into the bar, stepped up to Clements, and shot him in the face with a revolver. After shooting Clements, Bailey holstered his weapon, turned, and strode out of the saloon. Less than ten seconds had passed since he had entered. The few patrons in the Coney Island at the time remained motionless, stunned, for several seconds before someone approached the bleeding and dying Clements on the floor next to the bar. Moments later, another witness to Oliver Lee's criminal activities was dead.

Over the decades, historians have attempted to portray the killing of Mannen Clements, Jr. in a cut-and-dried manner and have labeled former constable Joe Brown as the killer. No solid evidence, however, was ever presented for such. Brown's alleged guilt was never proven in court, and the murder was generally regarded as an unsolved mystery until 2016 when the descendants of Todd Bailey came forth and revealed his role in Lee family affairs. (see "Background")

Mannen Clements, Jr.

35
TRANSITIONS

As time passed in the Tularosa Basin, Oliver Lee's status as a successful rancher grew. His cattle and horse herds made him a prosperous man and he continued to hold the respect of other cattlemen in the area. In many ways, Lee was regarded as a leader, and men looked up to him. Many were still suspicious of him having involvement in the killing of Colonel Fountain and his son, and others were entirely convinced of his participation. Though some whispering still went on behind his back, Lee was held in high regard by a large segment of the citizenry, and in fear by others. Officially freed of guilt by a jury, and now rid of all of his enemies, things were about to get even better for Oliver Lee.

In 1914 when Lee was forty-nine years old, he entered into negotiations with El Paso businessman and banker James G. McNary and several of his partners. McNary offered to buy Lee's ranching enterprises at a good price, along with those of several others in the Tularosa Basin. McNary desired to create a giant cattle raising operation with Lee as the manager. Lee agreed to the proposition. A corporation was formed with McNary as president and Lee as vice-president and general manager. The ranch was to be named the Circle Cross and headquarters were established on the Sacramento River in the nearby mountains. In a short time, the Circle Cross brand was registered and the operation was underway.

The Circle Cross ranching enterprise continued to grow. Ranches were bought up as fast as possible. The Circle Cross covered an area from the Mescalero Indian Reservation near Ruidoso south to Ysleta, Texas, and from the Tularosa Basin to the Cornudas Mountains. The Circle Cross eventually grew to one million acres, and was the largest ranch in southern

New Mexico. Though occasionally hampered by drought and a sometimes fickle market, the ranch thrived.

The headquarters in the Sacramento Mountains was regarded as a showplace, and it was there that real and potential buyers of cattle and horses were wined, dined, and entertained. It consisted of a large house and barn, corrals, an orchard and garden, and even a deer park. Business was good for the Circle Cross and life improved for all connected with it, especially Oliver Lee, but the end was approaching.

The Circle Cross was beset with the usual difficulties associated with a large ranching empire: weather, economics, and more. The downhill slide began, however, when McNary's First National Bank of El Paso ran into difficulties and was on the brink of failure. When it finally crashed, it took McNary's First Mortgage Company with it.

At one point, the ranch had purchased 10,000 head of cattle from a Marfa, Texas, rancher for $800,000. The herd was driven to a region near the Sacramento Mountains, but because of a recent drought there was not enough grass to sustain it. The cattle were shipped to pastures in Montana and North Dakota and arrived just in time to be greeted by another drought in that area. Desperate, the herd was then transported to Kansas where they were put up for sale at a time when the market for beef dropped to a frightening low. The cattle were sold and, though the Circle Cross recovered its expenses, it lost the original $800,000 investment. This situation, along with the ongoing drought and drop in cattle prices, as well as the difficulties associated with McNary's bank and mortgage company, spelled ruin for the Circle Cross.

Since Oliver Lee had invested a great deal of his own money into the Circle Cross, he lost heavily. He did manage, however, to take possession of the Circle Cross headquarters, which he turned into his own residence. Unfortunately, he was later forced to sell it. An El Paso man named Lee Orndorff handled the sale. As it turned out, the sale of the house and property proved to be more difficult than expected.

Author Sonnichsen provided an explanation. He related that when Lee asked Orndorff why it was so difficult to sell the property, Orndorff responded by saying that it was because of Lee's reputation, that potentially interested buyers feared that Lee would shoot them if they set foot on the place. Lee was horrified at this explanation, and told Orndorff that he had never caused harm to anyone "unless they hurt me first. Then I made them pay." The house and property was eventually sold to a physician.

Since the Fountain trial in Hillsboro, New Mexico, in 1899, Oliver Lee rarely spoke of the case, and during the few times he did, he denied having any role in the abduction or murders or being aware of anyone else who might have been involved with them.

Oliver Milton Lee

36
POLITICS

By 1914, Oliver Lee had accomplished a great deal during his lifetime. He was forty-nine-years-old and had experienced success as a rancher and businessman. As a known livestock rustler and killer, he had successfully evaded conviction, in large part with the help of his adept lawyer and co-conspirator, Albert B. Fall. With his ranching days behind him, and with his enemies vanquished, Lee settled into semi-retirement at his home in Alamogordo. For a time, he struggled with the unaccustomed idleness, and it wasn't long before he found something else to do. He decided to enter politics.

Lee assessed his chances of winning a political office and was convinced he could muster the votes to do so, many of them coming from area cattle ranchers who remained steadfastly loyal to him. In 1918, Lee switched political parties and became a Republican. He was easily elected state representative that year. He ran for and was elected for two additional terms.

In November 1919, Lee was invited by his friend Johnny Hutchings to ride with him during a cross-country automobile race from El Paso to Phoenix. A half-hour after the start of the race, the competitors were approaching Lanark Station west of El Paso when a bystander raised a rifle and shot at Hutchings' automobile. The bullet passed through the back seat and into Hutchings' back, killing him. On learning of the incident, most were convinced that the bullet was intended for Oliver Lee. The shooter was Major William F. Scanland who resided at Fort Bliss, Texas. Scanland was convicted of murder and sentenced to prison. While his case was on appeal, Scanland was beaten to death. The connection between Lee and Scanland, if any, has never been made clear.

In 1926, Lee decided to run for a New Mexico senate seat. He won, and won again in 1928. In 1932, Lee ran for New Mexico State Land Commissioner, but was defeated in what turned out to be a Democratic sweep.

Lee's time in politics was relatively uneventful; he did not attract headlines as he did in his younger days. Most of his contributions in terms of legislation were related to advancing the causes of and bettering the situations for New Mexico ranchers. Lee is credited with paving the way for a railroad line to run through Alamogordo, a significant development for Alamogordo's business and growth. Other than these few, yet important, contributions, the name Oliver Lee remained out of the newspapers.

37
THE END

Toward the end of his life, Oliver Lee continued to live in Alamogordo where he served for a time as director of the Federal Land Bank. He and his wife of forty-three years, Winnie, had several children. During the spring of 1941, Lee suffered a heart attack that left him weak and inactive. According to one report, Lee had a stroke on December 15, 1941, which left him in a coma. He died two days later. Oliver Lee was seventy-six-years-old. He was interred in Alamogordo's Monte Vista Cemetery, laid to rest near several members of his family.

In 1940, because of its historical, archeological, and ecological significance, two large tracts of land in Otero County that included Oliver Lee's Dog Canyon ranch and headquarters were acquired by the state of New Mexico. The land was later transferred to the State Parks Service. In 1979, Oliver Lee Memorial State Park was established. It is open 365 days per year. Here, one can hike, camp, explore the picturesque Dog Canyon and environs, visit Frenchy's cabin, and tour the former home and ranch headquarters of Lee. The park brochure identifies Lee as "a pioneer southern New Mexico rancher and state legislator…." It makes no mention of Lee's established role as a rustler of livestock, nor does it mention his participation in the assassinations of Albert Jennings Fountain, Pat Garrett, Mannen Clements, Jr., Les Dow, and others.

36

THE END

Toward the end of his life, Oliver Lee continued to live in Alamogordo, where he served for a time as director of the Federal Land Bank [illegible] and [illegible] Warren [illegible] During the summer of 1941, he suffered a heart attack that left him weak [illegible]

According to one report, he suffered a stroke on December 15, 1941, which left him in a coma. He died seven days later. Oliver Lee was seventy-[illegible] years old. He is buried in Alamogordo's Monte Vista Cemetery, [illegible] near several members of his family.

[illegible] magnificent, rich, elegant, and [illegible] significant [illegible] land in Otero County that included Dog Canyon ranch headquarters, were acquired by the State of New Mexico. The land was later transferred to the State Parks Division. In 1977, Oliver Lee Memorial State Park was established. It is open [illegible] year. Visitors can hike [illegible] Dog Canyon and [illegible] by [illegible] and [illegible] the former home and ranch headquarters of Lee. [illegible] makes no mention of Lee's [illegible] involvement in the assassinations of Albert Jennings Fountain, [illegible] Mangus Clements, [illegible] and others.

EPILOGUE

Most of the participants in the theater and adventures associated with Oliver Milton Lee and his activities went in with their lives following the killings of Albert Jennings Fountain, Pat Garrett, and others. Though some of them were still objects suspicion among many New Mexico residents, they encountered few law-related difficulties and tended to go about their business in a relatively quiet many, with Albert Fall an exception.

Oliver Lee

Though Oliver Milton Lee undoubtedly played a prominent role in the abduction and killing of Colonel Albert Fountain and his young son Henry, he spoke little about the affair during the remainder of his life. Further, though he, along with others, was responsible for the assassination of Pat Garrett, he never revisited that subject, either.

Lee continued to live in his Dog Canyon home, operate his ranches, and enjoyed some success. During this time, he was regarded as a prominent and respected cattleman. Eventually, he divested himself of his holdings and moved to Alamogordo.

Though Oliver Milton Lee is touted as an important New Mexico rancher and legislator, the fact remains that he was a killer of men. According to investigations, we know for certain that the men he killed, or had killed, included Albert Jennings Fountain, Pat Garrett, Walter Good, Francois Jean "Frenchy" Rochas, Charley Rhodius, Matt Coffelt, Les Dow, and Mannen Clements. Lee is a suspect in the killings of a number of other, less prominent, individuals. Several descendants of Oliver Lee continue to live and ranch in New Mexico today.

Jim Gilliland

Several years following the Fountain episode, Jim Gilliland purchased a ranch sixty-five miles northwest of Alamogordo. It was rumored that on several occasions throughout the remainder of his life, Jim Gilliland admitted his role in the abduction and killing of Albert Jennings Fountain and the killing of eight-year-old Henry Fountain. Initially, Gilliland bragged about his involvement, and claimed that everyone was better off without Fountain around. During his later years, however, it was said that when Gilliland talked about killing young Henry Fountain he cried openly and expressed regret. It was reported that Gilliland drank heavily in the hope that it would help him forget.

Another story that made the rounds claimed that Gilliland had arranged a meeting with a Las Cruces lawyer who wrote down his confession and notarized it. Further, members of the Gilliland family revealed that Jim had kept a diary that was filled with details of the Fountain killings, with special attention given to his role in cutting Henry Fountain's throat. The notarized confession, as well as the diary, is in the possession of Gilliland descendants who, at this writing, refuse to have it made public.

In 1916, Gilliland, who had assisted in burying the bodies of Albert and Henry Fountain in a remote canyon in the San Andres Mountains grew concerned that the gravesite would remain unmarked. Likely out of guilt, according to some, he traveled to the location and marked the grave with a large rock.

As an elderly man and unable to keep up with the obligations and hard work associated with ranching 63,000 acres, he sold his property and operation in 1937 to a man named Butler Oral Burris, who went by the nickname "Snook." Burris had known Oliver Lee and rancher W. W. Cox, and eventually became friends with Gilliland. Following the sale of his ranch, Gilliland remained on site for two months to assist Burris in gathering the cattle. During that time, the two men enjoyed long conversations, and Burris learned a lot about Gilliland's past and his role in the Fountain murders. Gilliland eventually moved to Hot Springs, New Mexico. He passed away there within a year. Today, Hot Springs is known as Truth or Consequences.

During a 1969 interview with author Leon Metz, Burris stated that Gilliland, at around seventy-five years of age, was in relatively good health, was very alert, and remained active, though he walked with a stoop. He described Gilliland as six-feet-four-inches tall and weighing about 250 pounds.

At one point during their brief relationship, Gilliland handed Burris a "Masonic pin, very rare...with an Odd Fellows link on the bottom of it." Gilliland told Burris he took the pin off the body of Colonel Albert Jennings Fountain. He asked Burris to return it to Albert Fountain, Jr. on the event of his death. Gilliland passed away on August 8, 1948. Burris placed the pin in a safe deposit box for a time, and eventually saw that it was handed over to Fountain family members. According to Burris, "The family traced it for positive proof that it was the pin of [Colonel] Fountain," and identified it as having belonged to him.

Burris stated that Gilliland admitted killing young Henry Fountain, that he "just got him by the hair of the head and cut his little old throat." According to Burris, Gilliland said, I can still see that little fellow, but dead men tell no tales."

William McNew

A longtime friend and business and ranching partner of Oliver Lee, Bill McNew was described as having "ice-blue eyes" and was "the meanest, most murderous, and least forgiving of the trio consisting of him, Lee, and Gilliland."

Following the Fountain incident, McNew remained in ranching, eventually moving to San Marcial in Socorro County, New Mexico. It was said that McNew brought bad luck to the small community. During his time there, the town was destroyed on two occasions as a result of flooding from the nearby Rio Grande and once again as a result of fire. McNew then moved to Ancho, a tiny community in Lincoln County.

Author Leon Metz encountered an odd story concerning McNew. During the late spring of 1937, McNew suffered a stroke and, as no heartbeat could be detected, was declared to be dead. He was laid on a mortician's table to be prepared for burial when he suddenly regained consciousness. Several days later when he was able to talk, he told family members that while he was unconscious he had strange dreams. He said he saw himself in hell and was "standing up to his knees in molten lava."

A few weeks later on June 30, McNew had another stroke from which he died. Just prior to passing away, however, it was reported that his lower legs had manifested severe blisters and the skin peeled way as though it had been burned.

Bill Carr

Bill Carr, along with William McNew, was investigated relative to the disappearance of Colonel Fountain and his son, Henry. Both men were eventually released from custody at a formal hearing. Following this, Carr was said to have had a conversion at a tent revival and allegedly became overtly religious. Shortly thereafter, Carr would advance to the pulpit of many a subsequent revival or church service and deliver testimonials that reportedly revealed his role in the kidnapping and killing of the Fountains. Hearing of this, Oliver Lee, William McNew, Jim Gilliland, and others began to grow concerned and debated whether or not something needed to be done about their former partner. As it turned out, Carr was regarded by most who heard him testify as half-mad and few paid any attention to his incoherent ramblings.

W. W. Cox

William Webb Cox eventually became one of the most prominent and successful ranchers in New Mexico. He continued to operate and add to his ranch holdings via acquired homesteads, railroad lands, and squatters' rights. In 1910, Cox and his family moved to Las Cruces so this children could attend New Mexico A & M College (now New Mexico State University). Between 1911-1913, he served as Doña Ana County Treasurer and Tax Collector.

Cox passed away of natural causes on December 23, 1923 and is buried in the Masonic Cemetery in Las Cruces, New Mexico, not far from Pat Garrett. (One account gives the date of his death as December 31.) He was sixty-nine years old.

Wayne Brazel

Following Wayne Brazel's trial in the killing of Pat Garrett, the life of the young ranch hand and goat herder became a mystery, most of which has gone unsolved to this day.

In October of 1909, six months after being found not guilty of the murder, Brazel came into possession of Harrington Well, a property located several miles west of Lordsburg, New Mexico, and close to the Arizona border. Brazel filed to homestead 160 acres surrounding the well and moved onto it with Olive Boyd, who was either his fiancé or his wife. In 1911, Olive gave birth to a son.

Olive's pregnancy had been difficult, and for the six months following the birth she fought to recover her health to no avail. She finally succumbed to pneumonia. Wayne, the widowed father of a six-month old child, was devastated by the loss of his companion and, according to what little information is available, never got over it.

Brazel sold his ranch in 1913. Soon thereafter, charges of perjury related to a former homestead claim were filed against him by the federal government. For reasons unclear, the charges were dropped in May 1914. Within a few weeks, Wayne Brazel made arrangements for the care of his son and then vanished. He left no word of his plans or destination with friends or relatives and to this day no one knows what happened to him. Reports filtered in over the years that Brazel died a natural death, or that he was killed. The reported places of his demise included more than one dozen locations scattered across New Mexico and Arizona. None were ever substantiated.

In his book, *The Strange Story of Wayne Brazel,* author Robert Mullin reported that Brazel's son hired El Paso attorney H. L. McCune to investigate his father's disappearance and attempt to learn what happened. McCune concluded that the "probable explanation" was that Wayne Brazel journeyed to South America to seek ranching opportunities there and was subsequently killed by the "Butch Cassidy gang."

Attorney McCune no doubt collected a fee for his alleged investigative work and the final determination, but provided little to nothing in the way of substantiating his claim. Further, prevailing evidence shows that while in South America, Butch Cassidy led no such gang and only partnered with his friend, Harry Longabaugh, known as the Sundance Kid. Further, nothing was ever heard from or about Cassidy in South America after November 7, 1908, a bit over eight months following the killing of Pat Garrett and approximately six years before Wayne Brazel disappeared.

"Killin' Jim" Miller

James Brown Miller, best known as "Killin' Jim," was also occasionally identified as "Deacon Jim" Miller because of his avoidance of alcohol and tobacco, never swearing, and his habit of attending church every Sunday. Miller was said to have killed forty men, but extant evidence can only verify twelve.

Throughout much of his life, Miller made his living as a Texas Ranger, a deputy sheriff, a town marshal, a professional gambler, and as a professional assassin. In 1909, he was hired by two men to kill Oklahoma cattleman and former United States Deputy Marshal, Gus Bobbit. It was believed the men had a personal grudge against Bobbit, but they were also desirous of his ranch.

Using a shotgun, Miller killed Bobbit on February 27, 1909, in Ada, Oklahoma. He immediately fled to Texas. Before he died, Bobbitt identified his killer. Miller was arrested a short time later and extradited to Oklahoma to stand trial for murder. On the morning of April 19, 1909, a mob of thirty to forty men stormed the Ada jail and removed Miller, along with the others involved in the killing. The prisoners were dragged to an abandoned livery stable behind the jail and hanged. Miller was placed on a box while a noose was fastened around his neck. Before he could be pushed from the box, Miller allegedly shouted, "Let 'er rip!" and jumped.

Albert Bacon Fall

In 1912, Albert B. Fall was elected to the United States Senate on the Republican ticket, and re-elected in 1918. As a senator, Fall served as chairman of the Committee on Expenditures in the Department of Commerce and Labor. In March 1921, he was appointed Secretary of the Interior by President Warren G. Harding. Fall's department was given responsibility for the Naval Reserves land at Elk Hills and Buena Vista, California, and at Teapot Dome, Wyoming. Not long afterward, trouble visited Senator Fall.

In April 1922, Fall granted Henry F. Sinclair of the Mammoth Oil Company and Edward L. Doheny of the Pan American Petroleum and Transport Company the rights to drill for oil on Naval Reserves land. Sinclair and Doheny were close friends with Fall, and the senator granted them the rights with no open bidding, as was required by law. During a subsequent congressional investigation of what came to be known as the Teapot Dome Scandal, Fall was found guilty of conspiracy and bribery. According to documents presented to the court, Fall was paid $385,000 by

Doheny. It was the first time a cabinet member was convicted of a felony and sentenced to prison. Fall served nine months of a one year sentence.

Upon his release from prison, Fall returned to his home in the Tularosa Basin. Not long afterward, Doheny's corporation foreclosed on Fall's property as a result of unpaid loans. Albert Fall died on November 30, 1944, in El Paso, Texas, following a long illness

Todd Bailey

Todd Bailey remained in the employ of Oliver Lee for several months following the killing of Pat Garrett. A few weeks before Garrett was killed, Lee made arrangements with the former lawman's brother to ship cattle from New Mexico to Louisiana. Lee sent Todd Bailey to accompany the herd to Haynesville, Louisiana, a small town near the Arkansas border.

At Haynesville, Bailey met with Pat Garrett's brother. The substance of the meeting was never documented, but Bailey descendants explain that it had to do with determining whether or not there would be any hostile reaction from the family to Garrett's assassination. The brother informed Bailey that here would be no response to the killing.

While in Louisiana, Bailey attended a dance across the Arkansas border in the tiny community of Ravanna. There, he met his future wife. Bailey returned to New Mexico for a time. While there, Lee sent him to El Paso to kill Mannen Clements, who threatened to expose Lee, Albert Fall, W. W. Cox, and several others in the plot to kill Garrett. Following this assignment, Bailey returned to Louisiana. A short time later on April 12, 1909, he married.

On April 19, Bailey was back in New Mexico for the trial of Wayne Brazil. Oliver Lee was concerned that Carl Adamson would arrive to testify and feared that his former accomplice could not be trusted to assist in the defense. Bailey was given instructions to shoot and kill Adamson on the road into town. Adamson, who was in jail for smuggling Chinese laborers across the Mexican border, declined to testify.

Following Brazel's trial, Bailey returned to Louisiana. A few weeks later, he and his wife moved to Dodderidge, Arkansas, a short distance from Ravanna. According to Bailey descendants, he was occasionally summoned back to New Mexico by Oliver Lee to "take care of some business."

By the time the Great Depression hit the country years later, Bailey and his family fell upon hard times and moved to Broken Bow, Oklahoma, forty miles northwest of Dodderidge. There, he ran cattle, operated a butcher shop, and made illegal whiskey. Todd Bailey passed away on August 3, 1949, in Broken Bow.

The Bodies of Albert J. and Henry Fountain

In 1896, Jim Gilliland and Bill McNew buried the bodies of Albert Jennings Fountain and his son Henry, along with some of their personal items, including two rifles, in James Canyon in the Sacramento Mountains. Here they resided until October 14, 1900, when the site was discovered. Two men—William Smith and Alonzo Greenwood—were hunting deer in the Sacramento Mountain on or near the old Gilliland ranch when they spotted a rifle barrel sticking out of the ground. When they dug the rifle out they discovered a grave containing two bodies—a man and a boy.

On learning of the discovery. Jim Gilliland went to the site, disinterred the bodies, and reburied them not far away at a location near Piñon, New Mexico. The reburial was hasty and inefficient, and with the passage of several more years, the topsoil eroded away exposing the bones, along with the two rifles Fountain had carried. The year was 1915. This revelation came from a man named S. D. Railey (sometimes spelled Raley). Railey's brother, Bob, was married to Lucy Gilliland.

According to Railey in letters he wrote to Masonic headquarters in Las Cruces, brother Bob stumbled across the graves near Piñon. Bob, unfortunately, felt compelled to make his discovery known to too many people, and a short time later was shot and killed by Bill McNew. (There exists another version of the killing, that it was over which of the two men had the rights to a water well).

A short time later, the remains were moved once again, it is believed, by Gilliland and McNew, with Oliver Lee being kept informed. The new location was on the ranch of W. W. Cox and near the old gate to Pat Garrett's former ranch.

In 1940, W. W. Cox descendant Hal Cox pointed out the grave of the Fountains to a boy named Tom Dayberry. Cox told Dayberry that after he is gone and if anyone inquires, he can point out the grave. Dayberry told ten-year-old Will Orndorff, who, along with two friends, returned to the site and dug up the bones. By this time, according to the description, the bones no longer had any flesh or hair attached to them. Some of the bones were placed in a box which was hidden under Orndorff's bed. The skull of Albert Jennings Fountain was placed on Orndorff's dresser.

Hal Cox learned of the desecration of the burial site and the displaying of Fountain's skull from the Orndorff maid. Cox went to Orndorff and instructed him and the two friends to rebury the remains. They claimed they did, though a story surfaced not long afterward that Orndorff gave the skull to his girlfriend.

In 1940 Butler Oral "Snooks" Burris purchased a 65,000 acre ranch from Jim Gilliland. In 1941, Burris asked Gilliland about the graves on the property and was told that the Fountains had been buried there.

In 1990, Orndorff and his two friends, now elderly, returned to the Fountains' gravesite in the company of three private archeologists and the Doña Ana County sheriff. The archeologists had notified the sheriff that they had been researching the Fountain case and wanted to locate the burial site and mark it. Interestingly, one of the archeologists was married into the Lee family, and it is believed by some close to the issue that he learned of the site from family members. The site was marked and all departed.

There is more. According to a private investigator who specializes in old west cold cases, evidence he has uncovered suggests that one or more of the archeologists returned to the gravesite, dug up the remains of the Albert and Henry Fountain, and removed them to his home. As of this writing, the issue is being investigated.

Background

For well over a century, those who researched and wrote about New Mexico history and the lives and times of Oliver Lee, Pat Garrett, and Albert Jennings Fountain, chose, for reasons known only to them, overlooked or ignored the role of Todd Bailey, a quiet, competent, yet dangerous figure.

Todd Bailey first came to my attention on November 11, 2011. I received an email from a man named Buck Bailey of Wickes, Arkansas. Mr. Bailey said he had seen me on a History Channel episode wherein Pat Garrett and Billy the Kid were discussed. Bailey mentioned his grandfather, Todd Bailey, and his connection with Oliver Lee. Bailey also wrote that Oliver Lee had Garrett killed and that Todd Bailey pulled the trigger.

This information was never part of the accounts or lore of Garrett's assassination, and I pressed Bailey for details. Following a series of email conversations during the following weeks, I learned more about Todd Bailey's involvement in the assassination of Pat Garrett as well as, to my surprise and shock, the killing of Colonel Albert Jennings Fountain and his son, Henry, as well as investigator Les Dow, and others. I also learned about Todd Bailey's role during the trial of Oliver Lee and Jim Gilliland. All of this was revolutionary information and I was, at first, skeptical. I asked Bailey some hard questions, even tried to trip him up, to determine if he was telling the truth or if he was trying to perpetrate a tall tale. Bailey, a retired law enforcement officer, provided all of the correct answers. When I asked how he came by this information, he told me that as a child he, along with his brother and sister, sat at the feet of his grandfather, Todd Bailey himself, as the old man reminisced about his youth in New Mexico.

I'm a fairly competent interrogator, but I decided to get a professional involved. I contacted Steve Sederwall, a retired lawman with county, state, and federal investigative experience. Sederwall was currently working as a private detective specializing in historical cold cases, and he and I had exchanged information and notes on the killings of Garrett and Fountain. I put Sederwall in touch with Buck Bailey—lawman to lawman—to see what he could find out. What followed was a series of communications between Sederwall and Bailey in which a wealth of pertinent insight and information into the killings of Pat Garrett, Albert Jennings Fountain, and others was revealed.

As an old man, Todd Bailey, living out his final years in Arkansas and Oklahoma, related aspects of his past to his children and grandchildren. Thus was revealed his role in the murders ordered by Oliver Lee, his past handed down to his family via oral tradition. The tales were never in the form of boasting, they were merely a telling of the facts of what had occurred. And the tales never changed.

So intrigued was Sederwall with this font of information in the person of Buck Bailey that in March 2013 he made a trip from his home in New Mexico to Bailey's home in Arkansas to visit with and interview the man in person. In addition to Buck, Sederwall interviewed Mike Bailey, a cousin, and Buck's sister Brenda.

Buck and Mike had not seen each other in thirty-five years, but they came together to meet with Sederwall to reveal long and closely guarded family secrets. Sederwall was the first person outside the Bailey family to hear the details of the stories related by Todd Bailey, stories that came down through different branches of the clan, stories that Buck and Mike shared with each other for the first time, stories that were identical in substance and detail.

Sedcrwall traveled to Oklahoma to interview Buck's sister, Brenda, who provided even more insight and information relative to Todd Bailey. In the end, Buck Bailey, his cousin, and sister, assisted us in the investigations and solutions into a number of western cold cases.

Once the stories of the Bailey family were examined and analyzed, they needed to be checked out, verified. We found them to be remarkably accurate right down to specific geographical and chronological details. Though Buck Bailey had never been to the site of Garrett's assassination, his descriptions of the road, the ridge, the arroyo, the logistics, and the field of fire were accurate and precise. Even the mathematical calculation relative to the angle of the second bullet that entered and traveled through Garrett's body corresponded exactly with Todd Bailey's position as described by

Buck when he fired the shot from 130 feet away.

We looked for errors, exaggerations, and missteps in Todd Bailey's accounts as told to his descendants and found none. Buck Bailey, a retired lawman with thirty-seven years of experience knows the truth when he sees it. If there was any hokum associated with the tales of Todd Bailey, Buck would have known.

SELECTED REFERENCES

BOOKS:

Bullis, Don. *Duels, Gunfights, and Shootouts: Wild Tales From the Land of Enchantment.*

Curry, George, and Hening, H. B. *George Curry 1861–1947: An Autobiography.* Albuquerque: University of New Mexico Press. 1995.

Gibson, A. M. *The Life and Death of Colonel Albert Jennings Fountain.* Norman: The University of Oklahoma Press. 1985.

Harkey, Dee. *Mean as Hell: The Life of a New Mexico Lawman.* Albuquerque: University of New Mexico Press. 1948.

Hutchinson, W. H. *Another Verdict for Oliver Lee.* Clarendon, Texas: Clarendon Press. 1965.

_____. *A Bar Cross Man: The Life and Personal Writings of Eugene Manlove Rhodes.* Norman: University of Oklahoma Press. 1956.

Jameson, W. C. *The Assassination of Pat Garrett.* Guilford, Connecticut: TwoDot. 2020.

_____. *Billy the Kid: Investigating History's Mysteries.* Guilford, Connecticut: TwoDot. 2018.

_____. *Pat Garrett: The Man Behind the Badge.* Boulder, Colorado: Taylor

Trade Publishing. 2016.

_____. *Billy the Kid: Beyond the Grave.* Boulder, Colorado: Taylor Trade Publishing, 2005.

Keleher, William A. *The Fabulous Frontier.* Santa Fe, New Mexico: Rydal Press. 1945; New Edition, Santa Fe, New Mexico: Sunstone Press. 2008.

Metz, Leon. *The Encyclopedia of Lawmen, Outlaws, and Gunfighters.* Amazon Digital Services LLC, Published by Facts on File. 2002.

_____. *Pat Garrett: The Story of a Western Lawman.* Norman: The University of Oklahoma Press. 1974.

Mullin, Robert N. *The Strange Story of Wayne Brazil.* Canyon, Texas: Palo Duro Press, 1969.

Nash, Jay Robert. *Encyclopedia of Western Lawmen and Outlaws.* Lanham, Maryland: M. Evans & Company. 1989.

Owen, Gordon R. *The Two Alberts: Fountain and Fall.* Las Cruces, New Mexico: Yucca Tree Press. 1996.

Recko, Corey. *Murder on the White Sands: The Disappearance of Albert and Henry Fountain.* Denton: The University of North Texas Press. 2007.

Sonnichsen, C. L. *Tularosa: Last of the Frontier West.* Albuquerque: University of New Mexico Press. 1960.

Newspapers:

Dozens of articles related to Oliver Lee, Albert Fountain, Albert Fall, and other principals, as well as descriptions and summaries of pertinent events, have been gleaned from the following newspapers:

Alamogordo *News*
Austin, Texas, *Weekly Statesman*

Weekly Austin Republican
Capitan, New Mexico, *News*
El Paso, Texas, *Daily Herald*
El Paso, Texas, *Herald-Post*
El Paso, Texas, *Times*
Fort Griffin, Texas, *Frontier Echo*
Mesilla Valley Independent
Mesilla Valley Republican
Rio Grande Republican
Tularosa Valley Tribune

Interviews:

Bailey, Buck. Numerous long-distance telephone interviews between Buck Bailey and W. C. Jameson, as well as in-person interviews with Buck Bailey and Bailey family members conducted by private investigator Steve Sederwall.

Burris, Butler Oral. March 1, 1969 interview by Leon Claire Metz, Rumsey, California.

Reports:

Investigative Report In the Disappearance of Albert Jennings and Henry Fountain, March 6, 1896–May 13, 1896. Pinkerton National Detective Agency. Chicago, Illinois.

ACKNOWLEDGEMENTS

A significant debt is owed to the late Dr. C. L. Sonnichsen for undertaking much of the research spadework regarding Oliver Lee and related events in New Mexico's Tularosa Basin. Sonnichsen visited with and interviewed men who knew Lee, both friends and enemies. Doc, as he was known to many, served as an inspiration and mentor during the early stages of my writing career. I miss him.

Buck Bailey, a retired lawman and grandson of Todd Bailey, the killer of Pat Garrett, graciously shared Bailey family history and assisted in uncovering the life and times of the assassin.

Steve Sederwall, a private detective who specializes in cold cases of the Old West, has a keen eye for detail and a talent for locating documents and information overlooked by the historians. Chasing down Oliver Lee, Albert Jennings Fountain, and others throughout southeastern New Mexico was always an adventure with Sederwall.

Laurie Jameson, talented writer and editor, was always my first reader and inflicted an appreciated level of professionalism onto my projects.

www.ingramcontent.com/pod-product-compliance
Lightning Source LLC
LaVergne TN
LVHW030920080826
845145LV00013B/2986

* 9 7 8 1 6 3 2 9 3 7 8 4 1 *